The Irish in
Early Virginia
1600-1860

For Jon
Enjoy this read!
—Kevin
Donleavy

Kevin Donleavy

The Irish in Early Virginia 1600-1860

Pocahontas Press
Blacksburg, Virginia

Also by Kevin Donleavy

Strings of Life
Conversations with Old-Time Musicians from Virginia
and North Carolina

The Irish in
Early Virginia
1600-1860

Copyright © 2014 by Kevin Donleavy

ISBN 0-926487-77-9

Book design by Michael Abraham

Printed in the United States of America

Pocahontas Press
www.pocahontaspress.com

Donleavy has succeeded in giving a new and insightful perspective on early Irish settlements in Virginia. This book will be of special relevance to those interested in genealogy and family history — it contains a treasure chest of information that can assist in breaking roadblocks with ancestors so far back in U.S. history.

This very readable volume spotlights the lives of the early settlers, investigating immigration issues in a critical socio-economic, political, and cultural framework. His probing writing style gives us a vigilant look at real people's history reminiscent of Howard Zinn.

— **Chas. T. Moore, Jr., M.Ed., M.A.**
Head Librarian, McClelland Irish Library,
Irish Cultural and Learning Foundation,
Phoenix, Arizona

In the forty-odd years I have known the author, to say that he has been motivated by a passion for Irish history, culture and politics would be a gross understatement. This fact is reflected by his most recent work. The research and attention he has paid to such rarely addressed topics as forced emigration from Ireland, the relationship of Jefferson to United Irishmen exiles, and the Herculean and dangerous labors of the Irish workers on Virginia railroads is groundbreaking. And that is but part of the story. There should be a book like this for each of the States.

— **Seoirse MacDomhnaill, Irish Republican**
Movement (Official)

This is an invaluable and passionately researched book into the Irish Virginia connection. Going through Donleavy's lines, I start to feel weak in the stomach at the treatment of the Irish and American slaves in Barbados and Virginia. What makes the writing more poignant is to think that never in the history of the world have there been more slaves than the present day.

— **Paudy Scully, Irish author of *I Forgive Them All : The Judgement of John Twiss* and *The Turbulent Times and Travels of Peter MacAuliffe***

Kevin's book is a fascinating read with stories of early Irish immigrants who settled in America, and Virginia in particular. Kevin's knowledge of Irish history informs us that they brought little in their pockets, but very much in their hearts and minds. Of the thousands of well-documented names, most are not highlighted in our history books, but all contributed to the fabric of America that we enjoy today. Any history buff will delight in the many historical excerpts from many sources that are woven into this book. Any genealogist will appreciate the detailed exhaustive work done. All of us are inspired to learn just a little bit more of our own family's story.

— **Daniel Burke, of Clann Mhor research group (www.ClannMhor.org)**

*Indeed, in this remarkable, carefully written
account, the reader can trace the influences
Ireland has had on the history of Virginia from
the seventeenth century onward. One has only to
examine a roadmap to notice the impact – Irish
place-names are everywhere. Putting geography
aside, this book hones in on the human saga of
Irish influence on the state's historic development.
From political refugee and indentured slave to
aspiring citizen in a new world, the impact of the
Irish is both heartbreaking and awe inspiring.
Canal builder, railway worker, and farm labourer,
all contributed much, but so did the academic, the
business leader, and the skilled tradesman – each
eager to shape and build a new land. Through
determined research and careful study, Professor
Donleavy has constructed a detailed accounting of
the social/cultural/political impact the Irish made
in Virginia. If you are of Irish heritage, you'll find
your story within these pages.*

— **Cathal Liam, historical novelist, *Fear Not
the Storm: The Story of Tom Cullen, An
Irish Revolutionary***

A WORD OF THANKS

$\mathcal{I}$t is a pleasure to extend some words of gratitude to those who have encouraged this research project. Some individuals made suggestions which led to valuable discoveries. Local librarians and archivists made available useful sources in their organizations.

ABROAD: Bernard Browne in Enniscorthy, Raymond O'Sullivan in Newmarket, Tim Browne in Kanturk, Nellie Weldon in Ballyfermot, Joe McGowan of Mullaghmore in County Sligo, Paudy Scully of Newmarket and Herxheim, and all at Tí Chulainn in South Armagh.

STATESIDE: George McDonald, writer Cathal Liam, William Watson and Frank Watson, Dan Burke, Rhonda Roebuck, Michael Brittingham, Marjorie Maxey, Gertrude Weber, Stephen Brighton,Rich and Kathleen Lange, Douglas MacLeod, Marie Moriarty, Ruiseil Gray, historian Brian McGinn RIP, Beth Benedetto, Phil and Jo Ann England, Mary Kegley, Kate Kane and Bob Hickey, Mike Carruth, Mike Owen, Michael Kunzinger, my publishers Michael and Jane Abraham and Mary Holliman RIP, Tyler Burke, K. Edward Lay, Billy Mulligan, Lori Madden, Bill Tetzeli, John Gill (editor of *North Atlantic Review*), and comradely friends in Madison, Wisconsin.

Robert Hitchings of the Norfolk Library, Albemarle Historical Society, International Center for Jefferson Studies, Blue Ridge Irish Music School in Charlottesville, Clann Mhor research group, O'Neill-Malcom branch of Comhaltas Ceoltoiri Eireann, Jones Memorial Library of Lynchburg, Irish American Society of Richmond, Virginia Canals and Navigation Society, Mac Beard of the C & O Historical Society in Clifton Forge, and Byron Fraidley at Alleghany Historical Society in Covington.

The initial research for this book was supported by a grant from the Virginia Foundation for the Humanities.

Contents

The Irish in Early Virginia 1600-1860

Introduction

$\mathcal{H}$istorians have generally subscribed to the view that Virginia was settled, in the main, by considerable numbers of immigrants from England, Germany, and Scots Ulster. This position, however, tends to ignore the consideration that the Irish, although in much smaller numbers, played a definitive role in the evolution of the state.

Vast numbers of people born in Ireland have arrived in the New World over the past four centuries. In the estimation of historian Kerby Miller, "from the earliest seventeenth century to the establishment of the Irish Free State in 1921-1922, as many as seven million people emigrated from Ireland to North America."[1]

Many came as political refugees; many more were brought as indentured servants. The vast majority were fleeing a life of oppression and poverty, only to find an incredibly harsh life awaiting them.

In the early years, treatment meted out to African slaves and Irish servants was unspeakably vile, whether on the West Indies plantations or the Virginia plantations. Africans were trapped in slavery their entire lives. The majority of indentured servants "died without ever having a decent chance for survival" (historian Abbot Smith).[2]

A close look at present-day Virginia maps reveals some ninety or more Irish place-names around the state. From Burke's Corner, Doylesville, Foley Hill, and Gallihue Mountain; to Kinsale, Irish Creek, Lynchburg, and Shannon Hill ; and in such places as Richmond, Norfolk, Winchester, and Charlottesville, Irish immigrants made themselves felt in the Eastern Shore, the Piedmont, and the mountains.

In more than thirty counties, courthouse records indicate a profusion of Irish who obtained land in the 1600s and 1700s. From Accomack and Amherst and Buckingham, to Nansemond, Wythe, and Rockingham, thousands of individuals and couples acquired a hundred acres here or three hundred acres there, and cleared and farmed and established a new world for themselves. Their surnames are nearly uncountable: Hogan, Flynn, O'Sullivan, Grady, Quigley, McCarty, Farrell, O'Connor, Cavanagh, O'Brien, Riley, Kelly, Flanagan, Quinn, Nolan, O'Keefe, Geary, and McBride.

In time, some rose to political prominence. At least two state governors were of Irish background. During the 1700s some seventeen men of Irish extraction became county magistrates. A secretary of state was Joseph Lawless. A mayor of Richmond was Carleton McCarthy. John Lynch, son of Irishborn Charles, founded Lynchburg. John Lewis, born in Ireland in 1678, became the founder of Staunton town.

Some Irish communities were quite small, but larger concentrations came together in Charlottesville, Norfolk, Lynchburg, and Richmond. The Irish in these places lived and worked in relative harmony with their neighbors of other backgrounds, whether English, Scots Ulsterite, German, or Welsh. Much of the state's infrastructure of canals, roads, railways, and tunnels was built by the Irish in the nineteenth century.

The role of Irish immigrants in Virginia has been that of all ethnic groups that come to America. Individuals seek their own improvement as they add to the growth and improvement of society as a whole.

It can now be said that Irish individuals and their ideas had an impact on Thomas Jefferson. The "sage of Monticello" devoted a part of his library to Irish history, as detailed in the Charlottesville chapter. Research for this book has drawn a new conclusion concerning his political thought; that is, that Jefferson understood and supported the 1790s liberation movement waged by the Society of United Irishmen against the English administration in Ireland. His dislike and distrust of the English government supported his connections with such prominent United Irishmen as Burk, Sampson, MacNeven, and the Emmets. These political exiles in America wrote about the Rising of 1798 in Ireland. Jefferson wrote to two of them, Sampson and MacNeven, saying in effect "our struggle is your struggle."

Readers of these pages will be quick to notice a reliance on Irish surnames. The writer does not pretend to answer that question so tantalizing to historians and ethnographers: Did many Irish change their names in America ? Did an O'Halloran make himself or herself a Roberts, say, or a Blankenship, in trying to anticipate and avoid possible problems in this new world ?

The emphasis in this study is upon those of Gaelic extraction. The Scots who arrived in north-eastern Ireland squatted on stolen land for a few generations before moving on to America. Readers are directed, for historical background, to the "Servants ? Slaves ?" chapter in this book; but additional elements of that background appear here and there in other chapters.

Curious readers are also cautioned about Virginia county nomenclature. County names changed considerably over the years since the seventeenth century. The boundaries of Augusta County, for example, once extended to the Ohio River. In 1863, some fifty counties became the new state of West Virginia.

Two large infrastructure developments have been subsumed within two chapters. The 200-mile canal project (the James River and Kanawha Canal) is discussed in the Lynchburg pages, and the railroad-and-tunnels project through the Blue Ridge Mountains is examined in the Charlottesville chapter. Both undertakings were staffed by large numbers of Irish immigrants and African-American slaves.

It is hoped that readers will see parallels in the Irish and African-American situations in Virginia history (and indeed in the rest of America as well).

This study is in truth a work of Cultural Analysis. The writer has undertaken to depict the arrival of Irish people and their collective developed life in some communities. The writer has chosen to side with those in the "free" world who have suffered immeasurably. He agrees with that enlightened Englishman who wrote in 1746, "The poor people in Ireland are used worse than Negroes by their lords and masters."[3] He also agrees with another progressive English commentator in 1848:

> *I have visited the wasted remnants of the once noble Red Man on his reservation grounds in North America, and explored the "Negro Quarter" of the degraded and enslaved African. But never have I seen misery so intense, or physical degradation so complete, as among the dwellers of Ireland.*[4]

Endnotes

1. Kerby Miller, *Emigrants and Exiles: Ireland and the Irish Exodus to North America* (Oxford: University Press, 1985), p. 3.
2. Abbot E. Smith, *Colonists in Bondage: White Servitude and Convict Labor in America 1607-1776* (Gloucester, Mass.:Peter Smith, 1965), p. 60.
3. Lord Chesterfield, cited in Kevin Whelan, "The Green Atlantic," p. 233, in Kathleen Wilson, ed., *A New Imperial History: Culture, Identity and Modernity in Britain and the Empire, 1660-1840* (Cambridge: University Press, 2004).
4. James Hack Tuke, *A Visit to Connaught in the Autumn of 1847* (London: Ridgway, 1847), p. 17.

CHAPTER 1

Early Irish: Servants? or Slaves?

> The system of white servitude was cruel, to our
> modern way of thinking, because it subjected
> large numbers of persons to an exceedingly
> hard, laborious, and dangerous way of life, in
> strange regions and difficult climates. ...they
> were subjected to masters who often exploited
> them, and they were constrained by the whole
> machinery of colonial law to keep at their tasks,
> even if it killed them.

— Abbot E. Smith, *Colonists in Bondage*, pp. 303-4

There are two major ways of looking at the question of whether Irish immigrants became servants or slaves, the literal and the figurative. Let us look at the seventeenth-century situation of the Irish in Virginia and the West Indies islands.

In his widely-accepted study, *Colonists in Bondage*, historian Abbot Smith presumably clears the air by asserting that "there was never any such thing as perpetual slavery for any white man in any English colony."[1]

Kate McCafferty agrees with Smith, but only to a point. She focuses on Barbados of the mid-1600s in her engrossing novel, *Testimony of an Irish Slave Girl*. In the Preface, she points out, "Africans were stolen to become bondsmen in perpetuity, while Europeans were stolen to be indentured for a finite period."[2] Elaborating on Ireland of that era, she notes that "the requisite labor force was available at L3 [pounds] to L5 [pounds] a head, payable to the mercantile companies whose ships transplanted the kidnapped, trepanned, or exiled slaves.

> *And slaves they were. The usual initial indenture was for a period of seven years, after sale in Barbados. During this period of time, the indentured's master determined the amount of food to be given, when and if medical attention would be called for, and what sort of corporal punishment would be meted out...*

While scholars have argued that the bodies of slaves belonged to their master while only the labor of indentureds was his, noted authority on global slavery Orlando Patterson insists that this distinction "makes no sense whatsoever in real human terms."[3] Kerby Miller's arguments continue this train of thought.

> *Conditions were particularly harsh during the seventeenth century, when perhaps a third or more of all white settlers in the Caribbean and mainland colonies perished on the Atlantic voyage or during the first year's 'seasoning.' ...in 1676 Virginia's governor testified that in the colony's early decades four-fifths of the indentured servants died shortly after their arrival from the effects of disease,*

climate, or over-work. ...although mistreatment of colonial servants was common, Irish Catholics seem to have suffered especially severe abuse.[4]

Another respected specialist on the West Indies is Hilary Beckles. In reference to Barbados in the 1600s, he notes that

Irish servants and freemen suffered the most intense day-to-day discrimination and humiliation on the labor market. They were kept in slavelike conditions and rarely given employment that conferred prestige. ...English masters considered their Irish servants as belonging to a backward culture, unfit to contribute anything beyond their labor to colonial development.[5]

Let us turn to observations by Richard Dunn. He notes that the size of Barbados's population was roughly that of Virginia, and continues,

Some of the English and Irish youths shipped over in the 1640s and 1650s had been kidnapped. To be 'barbadosed' in the seventeenth century meant the same as to be 'shanghaied' in the twentieth. It would be hard to say whether...the Scottish and Irish soldiers captured in Cromwell's campaigns and sent over as military prisoners were any less hostile and rebellious than the Negroes dragged in chains from Africa. Irish Catholics constituted the largest block of servants on the island, and they were cordially

loathed by their English masters.[6]
"Cordially loathed" is a telling phrase.

Within a few decades, Barbadian agriculture moved from tobacco to sugar production, and Africans supplanted the Irish in the fields. By 1680, the island had some 13,000 Africans exploited by the English "nouveau-riche slave-owning gentry." Historian Dunn's overview is concise:

> *The rape's progress was fatally easy:*
> *from exploiting the English laboring*
> *poor to abusing colonial bondservants*
> *to ensnaring kidnaps and convicts to*
> *enslaving black Africans.*[7]

Audrey Lockhart sets 1619 or 1620 as the opening of "the trade in servants from Ireland to Virginia on a regular basis." His analysis of indentureship adds a bit more light:

> *From the legal point of view, their status*
> *during servitude was something between*
> *that of minors and that of slaves; they*
> *became, in law, their master's property*
> *until their time had expired. ...they could*
> *be bought and sold, bequeathed in wills*
> *or won in bets. Their situation has often*
> *been compared to that of slaves, the*
> *main difference being that the slave's*
> *bondage lasted for life.*[8]

In McCafferty's *Testimony of an Irish Slave Girl*, servant-slave Cot Daley's master loses her to another planter in a marathon cardplaying debauch (at the end of Section Two), and Cot grimly, stoically states, "Thus I was sold anew, for seven more years in bondage."[9]

What was the background of these Irish who came to the New World?

Estimates of their numbers vary, from 50,000 to 100,000. Only a relative handful were people of substance. Most would have been landless (the English had seized roughly eighty percent of Irish land by the mid-1600s, and ninety-five percent by the 1750s). The great majority of them lived at mere subsistence level. Some were deported for stealing food or for being vagrants or beggars or unemployed. Some were exiled for having taken up arms against the invading English military. And as Kerby Miller reminds us, "Before 1750 probably the great majority of the rural Irish, and many urban dwellers as well, spoke little or no English."[10]

Only a life of hopeless misery would have driven the Irish from their homeland. As Smith puts it, "It has usually been only with the greatest difficulty that people...have been persuaded to cut loose from their ancient moorings and try a new country."[11] Miller cites the expression in Irish, *Dob éigean dom imeacht go Meirice*, or, "Going to America was a necessity for me."[12] It was unavoidable exile.

These Irish who came to Virginia would have known of the horrors inflicted in Ireland by English forces in 1579-81 during the reign of Queen Elizabeth. Immense numbers of natives were killed by the military under the command of William Pelham, who made no distinction between man, woman, or child. In the words of Richard Berleth,

*Just to be Irish was a sentence of death.
...Pelham never ventured to guess how
many people were put to the sword,
but the estimates of Ormond and his
lieutenants approached 10,000...A rage
seemed to grip the English forces.* [13]

Crops were destroyed, livestock seized or slaughtered, forests set ablaze, humble dwellings leveled. Wide-spread famine ensued.

Trying to avoid annihilation, the Irish country folk endured *saol crua* (a hard life), living hand-to-mouth, *ar an anás* (living in poverty), and *ar do choimeád* (going into hiding). Many Gaelic terms for oppression no doubt emerged from this era: *ausmacht, daoirse, dochraide,* and *cos ar bolg.*

Modern chronicler Berleth agrees with "an observation by the very great Anglo-Irish historian W.E.H. Lecky: 'The pictures of the condition of Ireland at this time are as terrible as anything in human history.'" [14] Berleth's own evaluation is that "the face of Ireland was altered permanently, and the estrangement of the two countries... hardened into a lasting enmity." [15]

A scant forty years after the 1603 death of English Queen Elizabeth, much greater devastation took place in Ireland. In the measured words of the Physician-General of the English forces, William Petty,

*about 504,000 of the Irish perished
and were wasted by the sword, plague,
famine, hardships and banishment
between the 23rd October, 1641, and the*

same day in 1652.[16]

Let us hope that Petty, thinker and scientist, was unhappy with the near-genocidal ideas of many of his English colleagues.

Fleeing the chaos in their homeland, many Irish took flight to the newly established colonies in the West Indies and Virginia. However, they soon came to see their employer-planter as the *tioranach*, the oppressor, and to see the grim reality of the adage, *Ní thuigeann an sách an seang* (The well-fed don't understand the hungry). Hoping to outlive their indentured time, they fought *teas na gréine* (the heat of the sun), *obair chrua* (backbreaking work), and *galar báis* (fatal disease). Elsewhere in this book we mention the destruction wrought during nineteenth century canal-building and railway construction by these diseases: *dinnireacht* or dysentery, yellow fever, and *calar* (cholera).

The Irish indentureds were landed at ports in coastal Virginia. Let us look briefly at a few instances of the situation in such counties as Gloucester, Northampton, Rappahannock, and Warrasquioke.

Among the eighteen individuals brought over in 1635 were three from Ireland: Dennis Mohonney, Redman Fitzgarrett, and Nicholas Welsh. Their transportation costs were paid by a Thomas Butler, who owned 1,000 acres in Warrasquioke (renamed Isle of Wight in 1637). Transatlantic passage was paid for John O'Drenne, Edward Kenny, Richard O'Harrough, Dan O'Carby, Tom O'Derruck, and Owen O'Lealy in 1655 by one Lt. Colonel Anthony

Ellyott, landowner of some 1,400 acres.

A lesser land-holder was a John Hampton (150 acres) who imported Edmund Walch and Teague O'Moulins in that same year.

Owner of two hundred acres in Gloucester County in 1655 was Colonel Richard Lee, who brought over Cormack O'Mally, Teague Flanny, and Richard Harratt.

In 1656, Matilda and Tabitha Scarburgh/Scarbourgh brought to their joint estate of 3,500 acres (in Northampton) forty-one Africans and seventeen Irish. The Irish servants are named as follows:

Jane O'Tire	*Henry Carey*
Horly Kanny	*Undell Illey*
Morris Kiffe	*Glannel Terry*
Orsell Derry	*Cillina Clinn*
Nella O'Lanny	*Dello O'Melle*
William Mory	*Gwallo O'Loffe*
Tirish Mogon	*Calleat Moore*
Hareo Kennell	*Morley Morry*
Mack William	

In the second volume of *Cavaliers and Pioneers*, we learn of more indentured situations. In 1672, Colonel Augustine Warner paid transportation for more than two hundred immigrants. He owned some 10,000 acres in the counties of Rappahannock and Kent. His certifying statement cites "twelve Irishmen but I have not their names in memory but some of them are alive."

Landowners George Jones and Henry Clarke

held patents in the 1670s for some 1,200 acres in Rappahannock. They covered the transportation costs for bond-servants "Teag, Darby, and Denby, Irish boys."[17]

The curious reader can easily see the names of hundreds of early Virginia immigrants who arrived in Virginia. Some 350 are cited: 76 in the 1630s, 47 in the 1640s, and 221 in the 1650s. Alas, we know virtually nothing about Katharine Cullaine who came in 1653, or Teague O'Fallon in 1656, or Dennis Mahonney in 1635, or Margaret Osheelivan in 1654.[18]

Michael O'Brien also assembled a list of some 219 land grantees in some twenty-three counties during the seventeenth and eighteenth centuries. John Flynn acquired fifty acres in 1646; Miles Riley, two hundred in 1663; Edward Fagan, 150 in 1712; Daniel Maher, 841 in 1727; and Anne Fitzgerald, 182 acres in 1758.

Historian O'Brien's exhaustive courthouse research in Virginia also led him to chronicle some 217 marriages in seventeen counties during the 1700s. In Fauquier County, Betty O'Banon wed one James Neilson; Andrew O'Bannon wed Mary Smith; Benjamin O'Banon wed Eleanor Ash. In York County, individuals who married include Martha Sweeney, Richard Toole, Ann Powers, and Charles McFadden. Orange County individuals included Sarah Fitzgerald and John Donovan. In Spotsylvania County, individuals included Patrick Connelly, Susanna McKenna, Joseph McDermeath, and Frances Sullivan.[19]

When newspapers began to appear in Virginia, they frequently included "runaway notices," submissions paid for by the owner of an Irish servant or African slave.

In 1768, James Clark (age 28) ran away from his master in Amherst County. A Walter Clarke was jailed in Williamsburg in 1746, "supposed to be a servant of John Campbell" who was a merchant near New London in neighboring Bedford County. Numbers of Clarks/Clarkes in those counties were, according to family lore, Irish-born.

Daniel Connor Terelaugh "plays the bagpipes, ran away from Miles Barrett, Bedford County." William Noonan, "native of Ireland," became a runaway in 1775 in Appomattox. Michael Kelly, "along with his wife Margaret, both of whom speak Irish," ran away in Bedford County in 1771.

Bartholomew Carney, at about age thirty-five, fled his owner/ master in 1770 in Fauquier County. Serving-woman Bridget Dolan became a 1745 Williamsburg runaway. A blacksmith called John Cartey left his master in 1739 in Westmoreland County. John Farrell was about age 35 when he ran away to Hobb's Hole in 1773; he was pithily described as a "convict servant, cooper, b. in Ireland."

Vast Augusta County in 1768 saw the flight of one Tim Flin "with his young and lusty wife, Anne." In 1745, Darby Foley "ran away from John Fitzgerald, King William County, seen near Hobb's Hole." Apparently Hobb's Hole was a clandestine hideaway for Irish escape artists. The town of Tappahannock is there today.

A notice appeared in 1760 to inform readers about John Murphy: "Irish convict servant, joiner, speaks proper English, has been upon the stage and appears to be the complete gentleman." (A joiner was a house carpenter.)

An older runaway was a Ned Barry, age fifty to sixty, who "has much of the brogue," and who disappeared from a Staunton owner.

There were runaways from other counties: King George, Fairfax, Loudoun, Essex, Berkeley, Westmoreland, King and Queen, Prince George, Hanover, and Caroline. Urban areas lost runaways, too: Fredericksburg, Alexandria, Norfolk, Petersburg, and Winchester. Some were listed with their trades: sailor, engraver, soldier, shoemaker.

In 1745 and 1746, several Irish took to their heels from Williamsburg: James McDaniel, William Quirk, Bridget Dolan, and James McLaughlin. Military runaways from the Williamsburg area included John Brown (age 25), John Johnson (27), and John Howard (about 30); their names appear to be aliases.[20]

Some runaway advertisements deliver a closer descriptive glimpse. Of the three males who "ran away from Capt. McCarty's Plantation, on Pope's Creek, in Westmoreland County" in 1738, the reader learns this:

> *Edward Ormsby, is a small thin Fellow, of a swarthy Complexion, and is a Taylor by trade; has a Hesitation or Stammering in his Speech, and being an Irishman, has a*

good deal of the Brogue.[21]

The fact that this notice was submitted by Augustine Washington reminds the reader of the McCarty connection to George Washington's family noted elsewhere in this book.

A 1745 notice consists in part of this longer narrative:

> *Ran away from the Subscriber, in Prince*
> *George County, ...an Irish Servant*
> *Man, nam'd Thomas Hoy, aged about*
> *41 years, of a middle Stature, with a*
> *Scar under one of his Eyes, and some*
> *Scars on his Head; his little Finger of his*
> *left Hand has been broke, and is very*
> *crooked; he is very much given to strong*
> *Drink, and lisps when he is in Liquor;*
> *plays well on the Violin, and pretends to*
> *teach Dancing; He took with him when*
> *he went away, a large grey Gelding...,*
> *a fine Saddle and Bridle, a light colour'd*
> *Broad-Cloth Coat, two check Shirts, a*
> *Pair of Boots, one brown, and one small*
> *black Wig, and a Pair of Leather Breeches*
> *patch'd between the Thighs.*[22]

The William Quirk mentioned earlier was described in equally colorful words. This "Leatherdresser by Trade" left Williamsburg,

> *and hath feloniously carried away*
> *Deerskins, wearing Apparel, Wools and*
> *Utensils, to the Value of Twenty-four*
> *Pounds, or upwards. ...He went away,*
> *...heavily loaded, upon an old CropEar'd,*
> *Flea-bitten, white Horse, with a Switch-*

*tail. He has a conniving Way of Talking, a
right Irish Palaver, to delude the unwary;
and has been a Pretended Soldier, in the
late Expedition to Cuba.*[23]

Then there was Katherine Russell, who left
Orange County in 1745:

*she is a short, thick young Irish
Woman, about 18 Years of Age, of a
red Complexion. She had on, when she
went away, a new brown Linen Petticoat,
and old Cotton ditto, and an old Cotton
Waistcoat.*[24]

An ad was issued of a very young fellow, Edmund
Butler, "a Servant Lad...; he was born in Cork, aged
15 Years, about 4 Feet 6 Inches high, of a fair Complexion."[25]

A master complained in 1746 of the loss of one
Patrick Carroll:

*He is a short sly Fellow, talks with the
Brogue, has black Hair, and is very
handy, either as a Planter, Ditcher,
Butcher, Gardener, or Carter. ...he took
with him a Pair of Leather Bags well
stuffed, and Plenty of Money, not his
own. ...He has four Years and a Half to
serve.*[26]

Let us say farewell and good luck to these
errant souls. Perhaps they were overworked and
vilified; perhaps they wanted to be free of all English manipulation whatever; perhaps they were (as
their masters did aver) lazy and up to no good and
blasphemous idolaters and the like. Let us hope

that they prospered and found contentment, free of the English connection.

The conditions under which they lived and worked drove African slaves to unite with Irish indentureds in occasional armed uprisings against the planter class in the Caribbean area.

Richard Dunn's study highlights the historical elements of these insurrections, while Kate McCafferty's novel focuses on fictional, possible elements. In the mainland colonies, Irish servants escaped their masters by running away, looking for a life free from hatred and over-work.

Elizabeth Sparks was a former slave when she was interviewed by a researcher from the Works Progress Administration in 1937, in Mathews, Virginia. "Plenty of slaves ran away. Sometimes they beat them so bad they just couldn't stand it, and they would run away to the woods. If you get in the woods they couldn't get you. You could hide and people slip you something to eat."[27]

Another ex-slave, Charles Crawley, was a WPA interviewee that same year; Crawley was born prior to the Civil War. He drew a parallel between Africans and the Irish:

> *Did you know poor whites like slaves had to get a pass? I mean, remit, like us slaves, to sell anything and to go places or do anything. Just as we colored people, they had to go to some big white man like Colonel Allen, they did. ...Old Marster was more hard on them poor*

white folks than he was on us niggers.
I don't know but two sets of white folks
slaves up my way; ...These two families
worked on Allen's farm as we did.

   They lived as slaves just like us colored
folks. Yes, the poor white man had some
dark and tough days... were lashed and
treated, some of them, just as pitiful and
unmerciful.[28]

Badly treated as they were, the early Irish in Virginia seemingly did little in the way of agricultural dissent or guerrilla action. There was no organized runaway movement, but rather the actions of individuals or very small groups. In Ireland, the agrarian dissenters were active in the 1700s; in America, such dissent occurred in the 1830-1880 period of canal-digging and railway-building projects.

In Haiti in the 1980s, a sympathetic observer commented on disturbances on that island.

   The peasants were engaging in sabotage,
'poaching' of trees for charcoal, work
slowdowns, and a variety of other tactics
that the peasants called mawonaj. I was
surprised by the peasants' adaptation of
this term, which I knew only in relation
to its original meaning: escape from
slavery. Its use as a rubric for a class
of tactics of resistance and subterfuge
suggested a reinterpretation of the term
over the course of a history of resistance
to agents of oppression (whether foreign
or national) against whom outright
warfare was impossible.[29]

Endnotes

1. Abbot E. Smith, *Colonists in Bondage: White Servitude and Convict Labor in America, 1607–1776* (Gloucester, MA.: Peter Smith, 1965), p. 171.
2. Kate McCafferty, *Testimony of an Irish Slave Girl* (New York: Penguin, 2002), p. viii.
3. McCafferty, *Testimony of an Irish Slave Girl*, pp. vii-viii.
4. Kerby Miller, *Emigrants and Exiles: Ireland and the Irish Exodus to North America* (Oxford: University Press, 1985), p. 144.
5. Hilary McD. Beckles, "A 'riotous and unruly lot': Irish Indentured Servants and Freemen in the English West Indies," in *William and Mary Quarterly*, 47 (1990), pp. 510–11.
6. Richard S. Dunn, *Sugar and Slaves: The Rise of the Planter Class in the English West Indies, 1624–1713* (New York: Norton, 1973), p. 69.
7. Dunn, *Sugar and Slaves*, p. 73.
8. Audrey Lockhart, *Some Aspects of Emigration From Ireland to the North American Colonies Between 1660 and 1775* (New York: Arno, 1976), pp. 62–3.
9. McCafferty, *Testimony of an Irish Slave Girl*, p. 81.
10. Miller, *Emigrants and Exiles*, p. 70.
11. Smith, *Colonists in Bondage*, p. 43.
12. Miller, *Emigrants and Exiles*, p. 121.
13. Richard Berleth, *The Twilight Lords* (New York: Barnes & Noble, 1978), p. 130.
14. Berleth, *The Twilight Lords*, p. xiv.
15. Berleth, *The Twilight Lords*, p. xiii.
16. Peter Beresford Ellis, *Hell or Connaught! The Cromwellian Colonisation of Ireland, 1652-1660* (Belfast: Blackstaff, 1975), p. 9.
17. Nell Marion Nugent, ed., *Cavaliers and Pioneers: Abstracts of Virginia Land Patents and Grants* (Richmond: Virginia State Library, 1992), passim. Two volumes. (Original edition, 1934.)
18. Michael J. O'Brien, "Early Immigrants (1623 to 1666) Collected by George Cabell Greer," in *Journal of the American Irish Historical Society*, 13 (1913–14), 209–13.
19. O'Brien, *JAIHS*, 13, 219–24.

20. Robert K. Headley, Jr., *Genealogical Abstracts from 18th-Century Virginia Newspapers* (Baltimore, MD: Genealogical Publishing, 1987), passim.

21. Thomas Costa, ed., *Virginia Runaways: Runaway Slave advertisements from 18th century Virginia newspapers*, 2006. Etext.virginia.edu/costa.

22. Costa, *Virginia Runaways*.

23. Costa, *Virginia Runaways*.

24. Costa, *Virginia Runaways*.

25. Costa, *Virginia Runaways*.

26. Costa, *Virginia Runaways*.

27. Belinda Hurmence, ed., *We Lived in a Little Cabin in the Yard* (Winston-Salem, NC: Blair, 1994), p. 30.

28. Hurmence, pp. 5–6.

29. Gage Averill, *A Day for the Hunter, A Day for the Prey: Popular Music and Power in Haiti* (Chicago, IL: University Press, 1997), p. xii

CHAPTER 2

Winchester

$\mathcal{I}$t seems logical that Irish immigrants numbered among the European settlers on Virginia's Atlantic coast in the 1600s. It may come as
a surprise to find a considerable Irish presence further inland.

Winchester was established as a town in the
mid-1700s, and the surrounding area as Frederick
County within a very few years. The county is the
most northerly in the state, and Winchester is less
than ten miles from the boundaries of Pennsylvania and West Virginia.

We learn from the recollections of William Russell[1] that this area was full of the Irishry in the
eighteenth century. The first jail, built of stone,
was constructed by Duncan O'Gullion and others
about 1745; the first jailer was Edmund (Edward)
Power. Three years previously, William McMahon
and other locals built a pillory, whipping-post, and
ducking stool for town miscreants. Quakers were
locating in the area from the 1720s, and some of
them were occasionally lodged behind bars for pro-
testing the French and Indian War and for refusing
to pay taxes to the Anglican church.

An early arrival was Edward McGuire, born
about 1717 at Ardfert near Tralee in County Kerry.

Leaving Ireland in 1746, he landed at Philadelphia, and soon came to northern Virginia. In 1753 he acquired a sizable land grant at Winchester, and before 1760 Edward came to own more than 6,000 acres. He was the first major financial contributor toward the erection of the first Catholic church in Winchester; in 1777 he became a Justice in the county legal system. As we shall see, the McGuire family has figured prominently for some three centuries here.

Our guide William Russell passes a related story to us.

> *Some sixty years ago was seen standing*
> *on a bluff, a small one story house,*
> *occupied by an Irishman named McGuire,*
> *an old revolutionary soldier; many a lick*
> *did the boys receive over the head for*
> *making sport of him. His wife was known*
> *as blind Molley, and was considered a*
> *good old woman.[2]*

A McGuire hotel was built in the 1760s: "Two long frame or log houses some fifty feet each, with an alley passing through between the two houses."[3] The house was situated on Loudoun Street, just off Cork Street (which got its name in 1759, no doubt from the numbers of Irish living in this part of town).

Local marital ties fill in more of local history. Of some twenty-one Irish-flavored marriages recorded between 1774 and 1846, eleven took place in the eighteenth century:

Edward McGuire to Millisant Doby in 1774

John Sullivan to Margaret Ware in 1786
John Conner to Elizabeth Barnes in 1787
Mary Hogan to James Cochrane in 1788
Patrick Dougherty to Mary Edmundson in 1790
James Ryan to Mary Harden in 1790
Michael Kehoe to Jane McAll in 1792
Bernard Fagan to Ann Varden in 1795
Edward McGuire Jr. to Elizabeth Holmes in 1796
Rebecca Farrell to John Karty Jr. in 1797
Mary Kelley to William McCabe in 1799.

Newspapers from the 1700s tell of some Irish from the area who fled the military: Francis O'Neal, age 28; Thomas Harrison, age 26; Jeremiah Hamilton, age 20; Francis Quinn, age 35; Nicholas Watson, in his 40s; Henry Mahony; and William Murphy. Another Irish-born man, John Allen, deserted Capt. Tom Lewis' rifle company stationed in Staunton town in May, 1792.[4]

On October 1, 1791, one Thomas Ryan, described as a "breeches maker," died in Winchester.[5]

There were some thirty-five ordinaries doing business (for the hungry and weary) in town and county in the 1790s, most being located on Loudoun, Cameron, and Braddock streets. Thomas Keenan supplied the financial bond for the owners of a Loudoun ordinary, and Peter Kehoe established bond for John Butler's on Cameron. John Brady was an innkeeper in 1803, for whom Keenan served as bondsman. Edward McGuire Jr. operated his own inn in 1806, 1807, and 1811. And William McSherry was operating his inn in 1815, with Nicholas Fitzsimmons providing the monetary security.

The small center of Winchester was full of political overtones. Col. George Washington used the building at the intersection of Cork and Craddock as his office during the construction of Fort Loudoun in the 1750s. The predicament of the Irish who had escaped English oppression by fleeing to the New World was well known to Washington and other citizens.

A Belfast man born in 1790, Adam Douglass, had his book, *The Irish Emigrant*, published in Winchester by John T. Sharrocks in 1817. Douglass had received two wounds in an Irish regiment at the Battle of Waterloo.

The book appeared in two small volumes, and was sub-titled *An Historical Tale Founded on Fact, By an Hibernian*. The fictional hero, Owen McDermott, exiles himself after involvement in action in the Wexford area during the the Rising of 1798. His father, Brian McDermott, has an estate in County Antrim, located "immediately on the shores which were washed by the waters of the romantic and beautiful lake, called Lough Neagh."[6]

Douglass married, lived briefly on Loudoun Street, and then made his living as a schoolmaster and surveyor around New Market, in neighboring Shenandoah County. His hero Owen comes to America, where he discovers that, "in Columbia alone there was true liberty, except in one instance, which it is true was a disgraceful one — that a part of the human species are held in bondage, and that of the most ignominious description, merely in consequence of their differing in color from their own fellow creatures, and being much less refined than they who pretend to Christianity, but still vindicate the base doctrine of slavery."[7]

Another political exile in Winchester was a John Barty. Our historical guide Mr. Russell brings him to light:

> There was one character I had almost overlooked; he used to be seen on our streets, generally known as John Napper Tandy. His proper name was John Barty. He was one of the thirteen hostages that were held in England in the War of 1812, and was taken day after day before a court-martial for trial, with a rope around his neck. He was claimed as a British subject and they were trying him for treason. [Barty was subsequently released.] He was a weaver by trade and many there are in town, who can remember him yet.[8]

There were at least two other Winchester Irish who fought in 1812, Natty Ryan and Jack Ryan, both of whom died in combat.

In Mount Hebron cemetery, there is a headstone inscription worth citing in full:

> Dedicated to the memory of the Rev. George A. Reed; born at Sligo, Ireland, Feb.13, 1766; imigrated [sic] to the U.S., 1787; settled in Winchester 1788; after discharging with zeal and fidelity the duties of Mayor of Winchester, Magistrate and High Sheriff of Frederick, acting a

*conspicuous part as member of all the
benevolent orders of his day, he was
called to his final reward with the just on
the 1st day of April, 1849.*

Historian Russell also reminisced in the 1870s about Reed, fleshing him out for us:

*There is a large frame and log building
[on Piccadilly Street] erected about
eighty years ago, by Rev. George Reed
who left Ireland for 'wearing of the
Green.' He was a coppersmith by trade,
but for many years was a Methodist
preacher, and one of the first who built
up the church in this place. He was
married twice. His first wife he married in
Ireland, and they had three children.*[9]

Russell's long life (1800-1891) allowed him glimpses of survivors of such Irish events as the 1798 Rising and Emmet's 1803 Rising, as well as the Revolutionary War, the War of 1812, and the Civil War in America. He gives life and color to two more locals:

*After the close of the Revolutionary War,
there were several old soldiers who
seemed to have free use of the street;
they moved about peaceably unless
disturbed by some of the boys. One was
Daniel Haley.... He would sometimes
whack the boys with a long stick about
two feet long, which he carried. Like
McGuire, he always swore, "By the
sprig of shillelah, and the shamrock so
green."*[10]

And there was on Braddock Street a building erected many years ago by James Mack, an eccentric Irishman, well known for his wit. A famous toast of Jimmy Mack was well known — it was,

Health to the sick,
Honor to the brave,
Amendment to the constitution,
And freedom to the slave.[11]

It is a touching sentiment, especially when we reflect that the English government in 1801 had forced into law the union of Ireland with England.

The Irish made their way locally. Some served as Justices: Edward McGuire in 1777, Lewis Neill as both Justice and Sheriff during that same century, William McMahon during the mid-1700s, and James P. Riely in 1843. Serving as Mayor of Winchester during the 1800s were George Reed, James P. Riely, and Joseph Gamble.

The city of Denver, Colorado, was named after James A. Denver. His grandfather Patrick emigrated from Ireland and built an imposing brick house in Frederick County, in which James was born in 1817. Patrick had taken up arms as a United Irishman in the 1798 struggle in his native County Down, and that same year he was obliged to flee for his life to America. He died in 1831 at age 85, and is buried in the Catholic graveyard in Winchester. James eventually became Secretary of State in California in the 1850s, and was elected to the U.S. House of Representatives in 1855. (Patrick is briefly mentioned in John Denvir, *The Life Story of an Old Rebel,* available on-line as a Gutenberg eBook, and also in James H. Bailey II, *A History of the Diocese of Richmond.*)

We can continue to reconstruct Irish life in early Winchester, first by noting the roles played by local citizens, and then by wandering through Sacred Heart cemetery in town.

Col. William McMahon (sometimes spelled McMachen), who directed construction of the punishment apparatus, married one Elizabeth B. (she was born about 1690). Their sons were born in Ireland: John in 1723, Richard in 1725, and William in 1727. The Colonel himself died in Winchester in 1749.

There was a Margaret McMahon, probably a daughter to William and Elizabeth, said to have been born in Ireland in 1729, who married a Scotsman, James Bruce in Winchester in 1744. She died in Bardstown, Kentucky, in 1804.

McKeon, McKowan, and McKewan are variants of Thomas McKune's name. This Winchester citizen lived from 1765 to 1814.

Capt. Michael Coyle had a "hatter shop" in town, and a silversmith was Philip Riely. There was one Mulligan, who operated a bakery out of his own house, and "was accidentally killed by his son, several years before the late war."[12]

Davy Hill was a town weaver, and a John Reilly was another hatmaker. John Fagan for a period owned the much-frequented Red Lion Tavern, at the corner of Cork and Loudoun; this two-story granite edifice is a private residence today. He also owned property on the south side of Southwerk Street. (He was born in 1792; died in 1882.)

Our guide Mr. Russell tells us of two residents of Cameron Street. Bernard Reilly (1821 to 1896) lived there, and owned some thirteen lots in the town. Michael Ryan owned another Cameron house.

Another Cameron neighbor was "an old Irishman named Neddy Burns. I think he was a Revolutionary soldier; he never swore... As far as I know, he was a very inoffensive man."[13]

James McCarty was a shop-owner. He ran a "grocery and meat store" on Boscawen Street.[14]

The James Riely who was Mayor for a period owned a town property that at one time was owned by a Joseph McCracken, no doubt an emigrant from County Antrim. Riely the politico lived from 1808 'til 1859. He was Clerk of the County Court in 1858, had been Justice and Mayor in 1843, and was a member of the local Bar.

We hear more regarding Joseph Gamble, who died in 1855 at about age 78:

> *an Irishman, a tailor by trade, a gentleman of very neat appearance and of liberal education, who filled many offices in the corporation, Alderman, Councilman, and at one time mayor of the city.*[15]

One of the headstones in Sacred Heart cemetery marks the resting-place of Hugh Brady (1834-1909), and the inscription reveals his birthplace as "Desert Martin, Innis Carin, Co. Derry, Ireland." At his side is wife Ellen, born in 1844.

Russell comments on the Brady folk with an anecdote:

> *The next house* [on Loudoun], *a stone
> one, was also used as a hotel, kept by
> an Irishman named Brady. At this house
> about the year 1808, was exhibited the
> first elephant ever seen in this town.
> The house was afterwards occupied
> by William McCherry, who married the
> widow of Brady.*[16] (Probably the McSherry
> who operated a town ordinary in 1814.)

Russell contrasts the efforts of local Germans (the Deutsch) and Irish: "The town was first settled by the Dutch, who are said to be the 'Salt of the Earth,' if so, the Irish certainly are the pepper thereof."[17]

Another citizen, writing in 1931, cites another bit of local history, the Winchester Academy, which was founded in 1764. It received its state charter in 1785, becoming one of the earliest boys' schools in America. It became Shenandoah Valley Academy in 1865, and was closed in 1939. The writer, David Holmes Conrad, notes that "When I was a school boy, something more than sixty years ago, there was a standing war of skirmishes between the Academy boys and the Potato Hill boys."[18]

Holmes attended the prestigious Academy, as did very few of the Irish youngsters. Yet he lauds one of his professors, "Mr. McNamara, an eccentric old Irishman who reveled in the lines and angles of Euclid, rejoiced in the sections of the cone, and the hard evolutions of spherical geometry."[19] McNamara was teaching math there as early as 1810. This school was near the intersection of Academy and Clifford streets, on Academy Hill.

The more we explore local archival materials, the more closely we approach actual life in the 1700s. County records show that in June, 1763, Darby McCarty and wife Hannah leased some 400 acres to one Job Combes, "at the foot of a Hill on the West side of Pasage Creek ...Rent of one Ear of Indian Corn at the feast of St. Michael the Arch Angel."[20]

The same 1792 newspaper which mentioned the military deserters included this notice:

> *Ran away an Irish Servant named JOHN WHITE about 22 yrs. old, 5'5" black hair. from Jacob KELSLEY, Shenandoah County.[21]*

More 1792 tidbits. Patrick Daugherty/Dougherty owned and ran a tavern in town. There were other opportunities to join the clique of tavern-keepers, such as this offer: "To be rented for 3 months or longer that well-known house formerly occupied by Mr. John BREADY. It will suit either for a tavern or private family."[22] Another pub opportunity arose:

> *The Harp and Crown Tavern. Florence MAHONY most respectfully enforms [sic] his friends and the public that he has taken the house in main st. belonging to Mr. MICHAL M'KEWAN lately occupied by Mr. RICHARD M'SHERRY merchant.[23]*

Also running in that newspaper was a notice of letters resting at the town post office for "John Boyle, hatter," and for Edward Powers, "the gaoler,"[24] furthermore,

The Subscribers to the Building of the Catholic Chapel are requested to pay up their subscriptions to Mr. Edward POWERS or Peter KEHOE.[25]

Insurance papers indicate that Kehoe had a policy for his North Cameron Street property in the 1790s, as did John Kean, Joseph Gamble, John Brady, and Patrick Daugherty for their properties on North Loudoun Street.

The papers of the prominent James Wood family are lodged in the town's Handley Library. On several occasions the family interacted with Irish locals. In 1749, Duncan O'Gullion received a payment from Col. Wood. At Wood's demise in 1759, a debt to Patrick McCarty was paid. In 1795, Peter Kehoe was paid for "shoemaker services" rendered to younger members of the Wood family. John Brady was compensated for "Lodging and alcohol"in 1803, but there was additional money owed to him at Brady's death about 1807. And in 1823, this family paid Fitzsimmons and Reilly for "Salt and saltpeter."

Handley Library, a distinguished architectural landmark, and Handley Avenue and Handley Boulevard are named for Judge John Handley, born in 1835 at Enniscorthy in the County Wexford. He bequeathed $1.5 million to Winchester on his death, although he visited but never inhabited the town. (Handley lived in the District of Columbia, as well as Scranton, Pennsylvania, where he died.)

Back to the prominent McGuire family. Edward from County Kerry apparently married several times, no doubt on the death of a wife. His first marriage was to one Susannah Wheeler; in 1774 he and Millisant Doby were wedded.

Edward McGuire Jr. was born in 1767 and died in 1827; in 1796 he married Elizabeth, of the highly regarded Holmes family. Their home, in adjoining Clarke County, was "Woodville," near Berryville, a few miles east of Winchester. They produced two daughters and four sons, including Edward III, Hugh, and William. Edward III bought the brick house at 103 North Braddock Street. Built in 1790, it remains in the McGuire family to this day.

William McGuire in 1850 bought a two-story house near Berryville and re-named it "Norwood." It is unique: " 'Norwood' is one of the only northern Virginia plantation homes known to have been constructed by Irish settlers."[26] The main house had been built in the early 1800s, and was called the Buck Marsh Farm. It was first owned by the Neill family, Irish emigrants who came to the Shenandoah Valley from Pennsylvania in the 1730s. Lewis Neill was Sheriff and Justice of the Peace for Frederick County; his grand-son, also Lewis, built the main house.

Hugh Holmes McGuire (1801-1875) was director of the shortlived Winchester Medical College, and he became Winchester's first "Dr. McGuire."

Hunter Holmes McGuire, son of Hugh Holmes and Elizabeth McGuire, was born in Winchester;

he lived from 1835 to 1900, and became the best known of his family by his appointment as military medical director for Stonewall Jackson. Hunter is buried in Hollywood Cemetery in Richmond.

Rebecca Holmes McGuire married one John Macky in 1815. He perhaps was kinsman to the "Jimmy Mack" cited earlier in this chapter.

More Irish surnames appear in local marriages between 1801 and 1845, adding more layers of Irishness to Winchester:

Sarah Ryan in 1801
Mary O'Connor in 1803 (Jeremiah O'Connor was bondsman)
Michael Doran in 1803
Elizabeth Madden married James Bulger in 1806
George Cahill in 1807
Dennis O'Connor in 1812
Rosa Denver in 1815 (Patrick Denver was bondsman)
Charles Flannigan in 1815
Joseph Gamble Jr. in 1817
Kitty Kennedy married Jesse O'Roark in 1819
David Farrell married Elizabeth Whollihan in 1822
Peter Doyle in 1822
Sarah Fagan in 1825
Elizabeth Conner married Spencer Riley in 1832
Patrick Brady in 1842
Patrick McDermott in 1842 (Patrick Brady was bondsman)
Patrick Conner in 1845
Patrick Moriarty in 1845

Lacrinah McNamee married John Dignan in 1846 (John Fagan was bondsman).

In 1900, the burials in Sacred Heart cemetery were catalogued, and were printed in Casilear's useful book, *2200 Gravestone Inscriptions from Winchester and Frederick County.*[27] Some ninety-five stones bear obvious Irish surnames.

A stroll through this graveyard a century later adds approximately fifty additional markers, for a total of roughly 150 Irish interments.

A few of these deceased were born in the eighteenth century: Patrick Denver, ca. 1746 to 1831; Michael Fenton, 1789 to 1861; John Byrnes, ca.1796 to 1861; and probably John McCardell, who died in 1818. Denver came from County Down; Fenton, from County Cork; and Byrnes, from Lady's Island, in County Wexford. John Fagan's life stretched from 1792 to 1882, and he was born in Templeshanboe parish in County Waterford. His wife, born Mary Ann Clark, was born in 1798 in Ballycastle, County Antrim.

Several Cork-born are interred here. They include John O'Neal (1801-1874); Dennis Sheehan (born in 1809, emigrated in 1837, and died in 1897, and who came from Glanmire); and Catherine Sheehan who died in 1897. Other Corkonians are Anna Lynch who lived from ca.1810 to 1891, and was a native of Macroom; Annie Fenton, 1824 to 1889; and Dennie Collins, 1838 to 1899. Of the twenty or so Sullivans interred here, some doubtless were born in Cork.

The Cork-born also include Nancy Russell who lived from ca.1814 to 1889, and Michael Russell who died in 1872. One speculates that perhaps our guide, William Russell, was of this set of Russells.

Other counties are represented in Sacred Heart. Born in 1827, John Doran came from Croaghbeg, County Donegal. James Nealis was born in 1803 in Donegal, and his wife Annie A. was born in County Tyrone. James S. Nealis, also from Donegal, was born in the year 1808. Catherine Keating, native of County Sligo, died in 1896. John Mannion, native of County Galway, was buried at the young age of 32 in 1847; his headstone, according to the inscription, was "erected by Timothy and Hugh Mannion, his brothers." Francis Horan, from County Tipperary, lived from 1825 till 1882.

Edmon Sullivan of Fenster parish in Sumerwick Harbor, County Kerry, died in 1852. And "J.O. Mowarty" of Kerry, wife of Eugene Moriarty, was buried here in 1855, when she was but age 25. Another Kerryman was Thomas Coheen, whose death at age 78 occurred in 1897.

Other surnames to be noticed on monuments here include O'Donnel, Noonan, Harrington, Purcell, Kennedy, Griffin, O'Connell, Nolan, Tracy, Maleady, O'Leary, Conway, Sweeny, Reardon, Mahoney, Donovan, Madigan, Kane, Murry, Reilley, Grady, Higgins, McCarty, Horgan, Fitzpatrick, Crudden, O'Reilly, McFadden, and McVey. At the completion of a walk through this cemetery, the thoughtful observer will realize that the small Irish community in early Winchester was composed of many clans and social strata.

When Adam Douglass and his wife lived in Shenandoah, the county which borders Frederick County to the south, they probably met other Irish natives eager to discuss his book, *The Irish Emigrant*. In Wayland's chronicle of Shenandoah County, we read of some recruiting in 1861, cited in a local newspaper: "A company of Irishmen, numbering about 60, has been raised and are in barracks" in New Market. The newspaper is full of commentary and laudatory remarks:

> *Virginia was the first to hurl back the tide of Know-Nothingism, and maintain the rights of Irishmen — they now gratefully and willingly will lay down their lives, if necessary, to sustain, protect, and vindicate her rights. We are pleased to compliment the efforts of Mr. Thomas C. Fitzgerald, a noble son of the Emerald Isle. Having served in the Crimean War, he is well qualified for drilling the company... The whole company are noble specimens of Irishmen.*[28]

Wayland mentions Powell's Fort, "a valley enclosed by mountains, near the center of the Shenandoah Valley." Early settlers of Fort, or Fort Valley, as it is popularly called, were of German extraction, but "the O'Neals and the O'Flahertys were Irish."[29]

Beth Benedetto is a fluent Gaelic speaker, and she sings beautifully in the language. She, her husband, and their three youngsters live at Star Tannery community in Shenandoah County.

As the following note indicates, she is quite interested in the early Irish in her area.

> *Just an update about local Irish influences. It seems like most of my neighbors with Irish blood have their roots going back so far in the mountains and Shenandoah Valley that their ancestors must have come in the 18th century. One friend who says her folks thought their Mooney ancestors were Famine refugees has done enough genealogy to determine that they were here long before. Our Catholic church in Woodstock was built in 1890 by Irish railroad workers, but their descendants don't seem to be here anywhere — it's thought that those people kept on moving west. So the stories are all blurry and nothing much in records, and particularly not whether the immigrants spoke Irish or sang.[30]*

Endnotes

1. Garland R. Quarles and Lewis N. Barton, eds., *What I Know About Winchester, VA: Recollections of William Greenway Russell* (Winchester: Historical Society, 1953).
2. Quarles and Barton, p. 21. Russell's remarks were made during the 1870s.
3. Quarles and Barton, p. 69. Russell's remarks during the 1870s.
4. Bowen's *Centinel and Gazette* — *Winchester Political Repository*.
5. Bowen's *Centinel*.
6. Adam Douglass, *The Irish Emigrant* (Winchester: John T. Sharrocks, 1817), volume 1, p. 9.
7. Douglass, *The Irish Emigrant*, p. 199.
8. Quarles and Barton, p. 156. Napper Tandy was a well-known Irish leader in the 1798 Rising against the English.
9. Quarles and Barton, p. 31.
10. Quarles and Barton, p. 153.
11. Quarles and Barton, p. 33.
12. Quarles and Barton, p. 73.
13. Quarles and Barton, p. 110.
14. Quarles and Barton, p. 133.
15. Quarles and Barton, p. 74.
16. Quarles and Barton, p. 69.
17. Quarles and Barton, p. 110.
18. David Holmes Conrad, "Early History of Winchester," in *Annual Papers of Winchester Virginia Historical Society*, Volume 1 (1931), p. 182.
19. Conrad, p. 191.
20. Frederick County Records, 7 June 1763.
21. Bowen's *Centinel*.
22. Bowen's *Centinel*.
23. Bowen's *Centinel*.
24. Bowen's *Centinel*.
25. Bowen's *Centinel*.
26. Virginia Department of Historic Resources, *Notes on Virginia*, Vol. 39 (Fall, 1995).
27. Connie Lee Casilear, compiler, private printing, (probably 1960).

28. John W. Wayland, *A History of Shenandoah County, Virginia* (Strasburg, VA: Shenandoah Press, 1976), p.296, citing the *New Market Spirit*, 1861.

29. Wayland. *A History of Shenandoah County, Virginia*, p. 182.

30. Letter to Kevin Donleavy, February, 2008. Beth and husband Peter have three children: Abby, Paul, and Clare. For a documentary film of Beth's singing and commentary, on the Web go to "YouTube Beth Benedetto."

CHAPTER 3

Norfolk

The eastern coast of Virginia saw a slow growth of new settlers in the 1600s and 1700s. By about 1650, Virginia's population of thirty thousand included some 300 Africans and about 4000 white indentured servants. While the majority of the settlers were English, small numbers of Irish (mostly indentured) numbered among them. Norfolk grew as the largest seaport and naval port in Virginia, and the Irish established their own lives in this new-world community.[1]

Early public records tell of land grants of the 1600s. Among the grantees in New Norfolk County were Patrick Kennedy with 600 acres in 1637; John Geary, 250 acres in 1640; Edmund Moore, 200 acres in 1657; Maurice Fegarrell, 200 acres in 1670; and Dennis Daly, 1485 acres in 1672 and 1680.

We can also trace the immigrants filling in the area by a glance at Norfolk County marriage records in the 1700s:

Roderick Conner married Margaret Scott in 1753
John Walsh married Patience Davis in 1754
Florence McNamara married Sarah Brodie in 1762
Ann Sweeney married Arthur Boush in 1763
Patrick Ryan married Catherine Lee in 1797

Barney Conley married Jane Long in 1797
Joanna Sullivan married George Lake in 1797
Richard McGrath married Mary Scott in 1797.

The Europeans came on vessel after vessel. In the seventeenth and eighteenth centuries, they sailed on such ships as the following[2]:

the Alexander, from Cork to the York River in 1654,
the Amity, from Ireland to Virginia in 1653,
the Unity, from Dublin to Virginia and Antigua, with 53 servants, in 1654,
the Golden Horse, from Ireland to Virginia in 1653,
the Fanny, from Ireland to Virginia in 1769 and 1770,
the Elizabeth, from Liverpool via Cork to Virginia in 1713,
the Dolly of Dublin, from Belfast to Hampton Roads in November 1789,
the Dolly of Dublin, from Belfast to Norfolk in December 1789,
the Molly, from Waterford to Norfolk in 1787,
the Mermaid, from Derry to Norfolk in 1789.
Other Irish ports of departure included Sligo, Limerick, Newry, and Killibegs.[3]

In addition to official records of land ownership, marriages, and sea voyages, we can also partly reconstruct the life of early "Irish Norfolk" from later commentaries and reminiscence-sketches, as well as the early editions of the local newspaper, the *Norfolk Herald*.

There are several extant editions of *Simmons's Directory of Norfolk*. The 1801 and 1806 directories are invaluable and very useful, with their listings of individuals, their occupations and trades, and their addresses.

Redmond Bourk, dry goods store
F.Richard Burke, auctioneer
Mary Creagh, schoolmistress
Peter Daley, "taylor"
Donaghey & Higgins, dry goods store
John Donaghy, shopkeeper
Daniel Dorney, "English Preceptor" at Norfolk Academy
William Dwyer, boot and shoe maker
James Gleeson, Borough constable
Joseph Hayes, brewer
James Herron, merchant
Walter Herron, rope and cordage manufacturer
Michael Lacey, "revd. priest of Rom.Catholic church, 20 market-square"
John Madden, "taylor" [sic]
Michael Madden, beer and porter house
John Mahan, house-carpenter
James McClenachan, merchant
Matthew McConn, bricklayer
Edward McGuire, Principal, Norfolk Academy
Joseph McKinnell, clerk
John McPhail, cooper
Hugh McQuellan, brewer
Bernard Mulhallan, dry good store
John Mullan, bricklayer
George Murphy, sail-maker

John Murphy, watch-maker, dwelling, 41 Fen-Church Street
Nathaniel Murphy, grocer
Patrick Murphy, tavern and boarding house
John O'Butler, sea-captain
James O'Connor, "editor of the Norfolk and Portsmouth Herald, office, 5 Fen-church-st."
Taaffe O'Connor, grocer and vintner, 51 Main Street
William O'Grady, "physician, surgeon and man-midwife"
Thomas O'Marra, shoe maker
Francis O'Meara, sea captain
Thomas O'Meara, boot and shoe maker
Mrs. Elizabeth O'Neill, widow
William Plume, leather and cordage store
Timothy Reardon, grocer
John Roarke, boarding house
Patrick Ryan, saddle and harness maker
Barnaby Scully, dry goods store
George Sweney, commission merchant
Felix Swiney, blacksmith
Edward Toole, house carpenter
Daniel Tracey, inspector of naval stores

There were others of Irish extraction in a close-knit area of some dozen streets and wharves. James Burke was another house carpenter, and Patrick Burke was a shopkeeper. Redmond Cody was a tobacconist at 117 Church Street; others on the street were Maurice Fitzgerald who lived at number 37; Thomas McDormand, a constable, lived at number 52; Elizabeth Murphy was a widow residing at number 74; a "Windsor chair maker" was Michael Murphy, who lived at number 97; Nathaniel Murphy the tailor worked out of number 98; number 2 was occupied by brick layer John O'Mullen; John Rourke or Roarke had his boarding house at number 72; Scully's dry goods shop was located at number 25; and Edward Toole inhabited number 26. Prominent citizen William Plume lived at number 73.

At the Market Square, locals could patronize Francis Lynch's shop at number 20 or auctioneers Horman & Burke at number 5 or merchants Allmand & Macgowan at number 2. Father Mike Lacey's home was also at number 20.

Main Street had its Irish overtones. Peter Daily the tailor could be found at number 124. At number 132 was the Exchange Coffeehouse. Joseph Hayes was a brewer at number 89. Taaffe O'Connor, the grocer and vintner, was located at number 51. Patrick Ryan's shop was situated at number 102.

Patrick McNamara, sea captain, lived at number 2 Rothery's Lane, and Dr. William O'Grady inhabited number 6. Nearby was Rothery's Wharf, where the merchants Burke and Roar or Roarke were located at number 11.

The schoolteacher Mary Creagh lived at 1 Boush's Lane. George Murphy lived at 10 Boush Street.

On Fen-church Street we find Mary Donnavon, a seamstress, at number 31. John Murphy lived at number 16, although his watchmaker's shop was to be found at 15 Water St. Also on Fen-church was the residence of sea captain John O'Butler at number 6. James O'Connor lived at number 5, and managed his newspaper the *Norfolk Herald* from the same location.

The premises of Redmond Burk's shop were at number 15 Little Water Street, at the intersection with Commerce Street. Across the street John Donnaghy kept a shop of some description at number 8. Sea captain Charles Mahon lived at number 10. Dennis McCarty ran a lodging house at number 30.

More Irish connections were scattered on a few nearby streets. Martin Doyle, described as "a trader" of some sort, was at number 1 Cove Street. The boarding house of Thomas Fitzgerald could be found at 11 Woodside's Wharf. James Herron did business on the Commerce Street Wharf. At some point journalist-editor O'Connor dwelt at 36 Catherine Street. Thomas O'Meara lived and worked out of 16 Bank Street. Grocer Tim Reardon's shop was located at 2 Water Street.

William Plume ran his very successful ropemaking enterprise at 5 Campbell's Wharf (more of him later).

There were numerous busy wharves in Norfolk by the end of the 1700s, and no doubt Irish and other immigrants found employment as navvies on Maxwell's, Hutching's, Newlon's, or the County Wharf. Early Norfolk had its Kelly Street and a Chappell Street. The Catholic church, with many Irish parishioners, was erected on the latter street.

We have a glimpse of a few individuals of Irish background, born in the 1700s, who died in Norfolk.

There was Captain Alexander McConnell who died in 1802, leaving a considerable estate, according to a notice in the *Norfolk Herald* of August 17 of that year. John Agnew, "a native of Belfast Ireland," was born about 1798 and died in 1841; he was interred at Cedar Grove Cemetery.[4] Born about 1761, one James Barry Senior died at age 84. He was Irish-born, "but for the last 50 years he was a respectable inhabitant of this Borough, and justly esteemed for his liberality."[5] James Herron was born in Wexford about 1770 and died in Norfolk in 1835.

Richard Burke died in 1802, and Patrick Burke died in 1807. Mrs. Elizabeth O'Connor died in 1811, and Martin Doyle died in 1813. The Reverend Father Michael Lacey (or DeLacy) died in 1815; that same year death came to Elizabeth, the wife of John Donaghy.

A native of County Cavan, Thomas Reilly, lived from about 1772 to 1845:

> *for more than 40 years a respectable and useful member of our community... by large expenditures in building up and beautifying the waste places within our borders; monuments of which he has left in the erection of a row of valuable warehouses on Rothery's wharf in 1845, when it was little better than a morass, and in the beautifully improved spot on Briggs' Point.*[6]

Elizabeth Furey, the "consort of Mr Patrick Furey," died in 1802 at age twenty-one: "In the death of this amiable lady, society is bereft of one in whom were united the best of hearts and affability of manners." (*Norfolk Herald*, Jan.5, 1802.)

In that last-mentioned issue of the *Herald*, a notice was printed that letters were being held at the local post office for many people, including Patrick Furey and some twenty other immigrants:

Michael Bourk	*Thomas McDivitt*
John Connelly	*Henry McDonaugh*
William Coughlan	*Jon O'Mullen*
Patrick Connor	*William O'Brien*
Thomas Dooley	*Mrs. O'Neal*
Mrs. Henry Dunleavy	*G. W. Sweeny*
William Gallagher	*B. Scully*
John Galwa	*D. Tracy*
Brien Gormley	*M. Tierney*
John Lynch	

The population of Norfolk grew from approximately 3000 in 1790 to roughly 6900 by the end of the decade.[7] The several shipyards and wharves were active places, as were the many shops. As observer William Forrest informs us,

Norfolk was a busy, bustling place...
There were very many foreigners,
principally from England and Scotland,
and quite a large number from France,
Ireland, etc. ...The houses were
principally of wood. ...None of the streets
were paved; and plentiful supplies of
mud and water in winter, and of dust,
frogs, and mosquitoes in summer, there

must have been.[8]

Forrest mentions several local religious congregations, and speaks of the funding for a Catholic church in adjoining Portsmouth:

> *In 1809, Mr. Patrick Robinson, an Irishman, bequested an estate to the pastor of the old church, which has recently sold for $7,750, and vested in the new church.*[9]

Early in the year 1800, John Rourke "of eccentric memory," opened his Exchange Coffee House. Rourke did his part to observe the death of George Washington. He hung a large transparency of Washington with this inscription, 'Washington in Glory – The World in Tears.' It attracted the special observation of large crowds of admiring spectators.[10]

At about this same time, the Norfolk Circulating Library boasted some three thousand books, which were housed on Main Street opposite the Market-House.

In the pages of the *Norfolk Herald* of March 3, 1803, are revealed some slices of colonial life. Patrick Ryan posted a "25 cents Reward" to anyone bringing back his seventeen-year-old errant apprentice. Peter Daley offers "Flannels," "Sattins," [sic] and "Corded Silk Velvet." Daley is looking for trade and promising that

> *Those gentlemen and ladies... can be accommodated with the latest fashions, and a suit of clothes in five hours notice.*"

Patrick Murphy opens his "Beer & Oyster House,

and apparently he will extend "satisfaction to those gentlemen who please to give his house the preference."

We read that there is a job opening for an accountant in the town:

"Apply at the *Herald* office, or to Taaffe O'Connor" (issue of March 12, 1803). Hugh McQuillin posts a notice a few years later (June 28, 1819) that he offers his patrons "A Supply of Excellent Ale, Porter, and Cider in bottles. He also offers for sale, 100 groce [sic] of Empty Bottles." His brewery apparently operated on the basis of an early recycling operation. Another establishment on Market Square belongs to Francis Lynch. He stocks hosiery, gloves, "Cassmeres," [sic] bonnets, "A handsome assortment of Chintzes & Calicoes," shawls, and "a few groce [sic] of excellent Playing Cards" (January 7, 1802). Charles Mahon advertises (January 5, 1802) that in his relocated inn and Porter House "a few Boarders will be taken by the week, month or year." Mahon notes that his business is now located in "that commodious house, lately occupied by Dr. O'Grady," and it specializes in "BeefSteak and Oyster Suppers," which can be washed down with "excellent bottled Porter, which he will sell on very moderate terms," as well as "draught Porter of an excellent quality, as usual."

Tobacconist, carpenter, furniture maker, tailor, brick mason, clothing merchant, innkeeper, teacher, watch maker, sea captain, grocer, shoe maker, rope manufacturer, sail maker, auctioneer, landlord, constable — all these individuals are Irish born or early Irish Virginians. They are intent upon making their way in a new world and carrying out their vocations and trades.

Joe McGowan, in his *Echoes of a Savage Land*, describes life in an early time in Ireland (and County Sligo in particular):

> *Footwear was not bought in shops but made by local shoemakers, of whom there were many in every locality... Tailors, boatbuilders, weavers, coopers, shoemakers, native and itinerant, plied their lifelong trades supplying needs as their fathers and grandfathers had done before them.*[11]

"Stop the Runaway!" headed a notice in the *Herald* of August 10, 1802:

> *Twenty dollars will be given as a reward... for securing JOHN CORRAN, an indented apprentice to the book-binding business. He is an Irish lad, 18 years of age, stout built, round shouldered, about 5 feet 4 inches high, jet black hair, brown eyes, face a little freckled.*

The notice was paid for by the owner of a bindery in Baltimore town, suggesting that Norfolk was known for its Irish residents. And it may be something of a puzzle that only a few years later there was mail awaiting a Captain William Corran at the Norfolk post office (issue of March 6, 1818).

Norfolk shops, whether Irish-owned or other, stocked a huge variety of goods brought by sailing vessels. There were barrels of beef, pork, and brandy. Shop shelves carried candles and candlesticks, firescreens, seeds, chocolate, tea, coffee, Madeira wine, salt, butter, flour, crackers, jewelry, rye whiskey, pearl combs, window glass, children's wear, looking-glasses, telescopes, soap, fruit knives, and various tools. Also available from the islands of Nevis, Antigua, and Barbados: rum, molasses, and sugar.

Musical tastes were catered to. One shop advertised flutes and fifes for sale, as well as "pocket pistols with or without bayonets." Its competitor, Niemeyer's on Main Street, advertised "Violins, Flutes, Fifes and Instruction Books, Violin strings, bows, bridges and screws" (issue of January 11, 1803; screws were tuning-pegs).

The political situation in Ireland of the 1790s drove some individuals to Norfolk. Let us look at a handful of them.

Richard Caldwell was born in 1780 at Ballymoney in County Antrim. He and an older brother John joined the United Irishmen organization, were eventually convicted of membership, and were allowed to exile themselves separately to America. According to family records, Richard "who had been reprieved from a death sentence" sailed from Derry, landing at Norfolk on September 1, 1798, along with other exiled passengers, "some young men who had been tried and sentenced at the same time with Richard." The two brothers were re-united in New

York state the following year. In 1812, Richard led
a contingent of U.S. troops to fight the English in
Canada, but he died of dysentery before reaching
the Canadian border.[12]

Michael Durey writes of the participation in
American political activities by exiled United Irish
activists:

> *"Keen to avenge the disaster of 1798,*
> *they were supportive of the drive for war*
> *with Britain during Madison's presidency.*
> *Many former* [United Irish] *prisoners*
> *fought in the war of 1812 and some died*
> *for their new country. "*[13]

A Presbyterian cleric, John Glendy of Maghera,
County Down, was interested in and advocated the
egalitarian ideas of the United Irishmen, but never
joined in their activities. However, when the local
United Irish seized Maghera town, he became a
marked man and fled to America:

> *At Derry, being joined by his faithful*
> *wife, he was compelled to embark on*
> *an old, unseaworthy vessel, crowded*
> *with emigrants as eager as himself to*
> *escape the vigorous persecution of a*
> *narrow-minded statesmanship. Soon*
> *after putting to sea, the passengers and*
> *crew were forced to man the pumps to*
> *keep the old hulk afloat. It was with the*
> *greatest difficulty they made harbour*
> *at Norfolk, Va., some time in the year*
> *1799.*[14]

Glendy served Presbyterian congregations in the

Staunton area a few years. He attracted the attention of Thomas Jefferson during his presidency,
and was selected as U.S. Senate chaplain in 1816.
He died in 1832 and is interred in Baltimore, this
thoughtful and articulate adherent of the enlightened notions of the United movement.

In the nineteenth century, James H. Shannon
(born in 1811) was a respected and well-known
businessman in the Portsmouth-Norfolk area. His
grandfather was Baron Shannon, "a refugee from
Ireland." According to Stewart's *History of Norfolk*,
Baron "was prominent in the Emmett [sic] Rebellion and for safety came to America."[15]

A man from Mountmellick, in what is now
County Laois, one John Shaw was born in 1773. He
was appointed by Thomas Jefferson as Navy Yard
commander in Norfolk in 1806. He had arrived in
Philadelphia in 1790; in the outbreak of War of
1812, he rose to the rank of naval commodore.

Mountmellick itself had witnessed "reckless
punishments" by the English commander there
in 1798. Although there had not been an uprising
in the town, nevertheless twelve local people were
executed, and many more were flogged nearly to
death.[16]

Thomas Aloysius Dornin was born in Ireland
in 1800 and died in Norfolk in 1874. He was a
reknowned US naval officer, in charge of the Norfolk Naval Yard for a number of years. Local historian Stewart remarks, "Commodore Dornin was a
native of Ireland, and his father was exiled in 1803
on account of his friendship with Robert Emmett

[sic], the Irish patriot."[17] The father, Bernard Dornin, born in 1764, was a Dublin publisher and bookseller, whose business was located first on Grafton Street and later on College Green. He belonged to the Dublin group of United Irishmen during the 1790s. After he fled with son Thomas to New York, he published (1807) a work by the prominent United leader, William James MacNeven, *Pieces of Irish History*. In that same year, MacNeven sent a copy to Thomas Jefferson; Jefferson corresponded with MacNeven, complimenting him on the book.[18]

One ship put in at Norfolk, Virginia, with over 400 of these 'men of '98,' and others scattered through a number of American states.[19]

This intriguing assertion has defeated attempts at confirmation by historians (notably Michael Durey and Brian McGinn). While the Irish community in Norfolk was indeed flourishing during that time, with scores of emigrants arriving, tracing those 400 has proved difficult. Possibly Wittke had in mind the fate of Irish politicals transported to Norfolk Island and Botany Bay by the English government. On the other hand, between 1798 and 1808 there were many Irish marriages locally, and some of the new husbands easily could have been 1798 exiles:

Frank McNamara married Elizabeth Haskins
Frank O'Mara and Francisca Martin

Walter Herron and Ann Plume
Thomas Moran and Susanna Hoggart
John Rourk and Mary Ritter
Margaret O'Rourk and James Anderson
Peter Daley and Elizabeth Miller
William Curran and Mary Ann Atkins
Davie Tracey and Fanny Butt
Nathaniel Murphy and Mary Preseorez
Bart. Broaders and Sarah Connor
William Ryan and Elizabeth Nichols
John Donaghy and Elizabeth Murphy
Dan Desmond and Elizabeth Smith
Patrick Quinn and Hannah Caslin
John Mahan and Eleanor McKim
John Deverux and Mary Metcalf
Thomas O'Meare and Martha Wyatt
Willis Daley and Mrs. Frankey Denny
Bridget Birmingham and Willam Harmer
Hugh Fallon and Elizabeth Russel
Terentius Keenan and Sarah Wyatt
Phebe Reardon and Edward Hudson
Roger Walsh and Brigida Madden
John Quinn and Ann McDonald

Let us keep in mind that many United insurgents from Antrim and Down were Presbyterians, and large numbers of them had non-Gaelic surnames.

Two Norfolk partners were Irish natives. William Plume and Walter Herron built a thriving ropemaking and cordage business in the late 1700s and early 1800s. One source notes that Plume (1756-1807) might have arrived in Norfolk before 1785.[20] Another source indicates that he arrived later,[21] and gives us a picture:

> *Mr Plume was a native of Ireland, whose real name was Moran. He had taken a very active part in the rebellion of 1798 in Ireland against the English rule, and... had to flee the land. ...For some reason, presumed to be the fear of persecution by the English government, he never revealed that he was the Irish rebel Moran until the time of his death. He was greatly respected and the soul of society, whose house was always open. His descendants of today are the Morans, Barrys, and Kings of the city of Norfolk.*

Historian O'Reilly noted that poet-songster Tom Moore stayed at "Plumesville," the Plume-Moran household during his visit to American communities.[22]

Plume's daughter Ann married Walter Herron in 1798, the year of his arrival from Wexford. At her death in 1833, Walter adopted a Wexford niece, Ann Behan, who became Ann Plume Behan Herron. Her own father, Dr. James H. Behan, joined her to live at the Plume estate after both Plume and Herron passed on.

The Plume-Herrons are known to the present day in Norfolk. In 1855, Ann "threw open her doors to the afflicted and cared for them until she succumbed to the disease herself"[23] during the horrendous yellow fever outbreak. The mansion soon became the Hospital of St. Vincent de Paul. (Some 2,000 citizens died during the period, including immigrants living in Irish Row and Barry's Row, the latter located on South Church Street.)

> *It has become the sad and painful task of the Junior Editor of this paper to announce the demise of his worthy and respected partner and co-editor, Mr. JAMES O'CONNOR, who breathed his last on Saturday the 3rd instant, at 5 o'clock in the afternoon. — Gradually bending beneath the afflictive hand of disease, during a period of several years, he finally sunk into the arms of death as into a gentle slumber, retaining all the faculties of his mind to the last moment.* (Norfolk Herald, Monday, July 5, 1819)

James O'Connor of Sligo was another of the many thousands of Irish who left their oppressed homeland in the late 1700s, searching for a different, better life in North America. He was born in Sligo Town in 1759, and learned the printing and newspaper trade in Dublin and later in London. A few scant details of his exile are contained in this obituary:

> *Finally he returned to his native town, where, with the assistance of a friend, he commenced the publication of a paper, co-eval with the commencement of the troubles in Ireland. Being inimical to the measures which the government was then prosecuting against his devoted country, he commented on them in such indignant and spirited terms as to draw down upon him the vengeance*

*of the royal party. The sequel may be
comprised in a few words. In those
days it was only necessary to point the
finger of suspicion in order to insure the
immolation of a victim. His printing office
was annihilated, and he, together with
all his relations in Sligo, was proscribed
and compelled to fly from the fangs of
despotic power. With a small wreck of
his property he procured the means of
emigrating to America, and landed in
Norfolk some time in the year 1794,
nearly destitute of funds. (Herald, July 5,
1819)*

O'Connor was at the desk of his *Sligo Herald*
office in December of 1793 and became co-editor of
the *Norfolk Herald* within a few months, taken on
as a partner by one Charles Willett, "an old and
intimate acquaintance."[24] They published together
for about a decade, O'Connor becoming sole owner
from 1804. Some pertinent articles appeared in
the issues of the Norfolk paper in 1802-1803 which
reflected O'Connor's political interests and outlook.

*The wretched condition of his native Erin
caused him many a sigh, and many a
melancholy retrospect; but in the land of
his adoption he beheld the benefactress
of his persecuted countrymen, the kind
and affectionate step-mother whose
open arms received them as her natural
offspring.[25]*

The front page of the Norfolk paper carried a
notice entitled State Prisoners in "The latest from

Europe" column. John Donovan, Thomas Johnson, and Joseph Burks had been released from seven months' imprisonment. The paper describes the first two men as "Irish gentlemen of great respectability and high connections" who had lived on the Continent for two years and were arrested in England.[26]

That same year the *Herald* printed a lengthy piece concerning Richard Musgrave, who in June that year had been seriously wounded in a pistol duel in Dublin. His challenger, William Todd Jones, had been vilified in Musgrave's book, *Memoirs of the Different Rebellions in Ireland*, published the previous year. Musgrave had accused Jones of having United Irish associations, a dangerous and potentially lethal allegation.

Musgrave had been appointed High Sheriff of County Waterford in 1780, and was elected by the local power elite to the Irish House of Commons shortly thereafter. He was an ultra-loyalist toward the English crown, and near-rabid in his anti-Catholic views. Historian David Dickson refers to the "sectarian outspokenness" of Musgrave's book, and labels its ethno-political views as "partisan rhetoric." Musgrave's views are those of the hanging-shooting-burning gentlemen cited by Thomas Packenham.[27]

Musgrave's hatred of the Irish is reflected in his relationship with his own wife. One night, as he supposedly was enduring a nightmare, he screamed at his spouse, "You infernal papist rebel!" and attempted to choke her to death.

In March of 1802, a small box appeared in the *Herald* that "Gentlemen as are desirous of celebrating the anniversary of ST PATRICK on Wednesday the 17th" could obtain tickets at the newspaper's office for the dinner event, which was to be held at Lindsay's Gardens.

Early in 1803, an article covered William Lindsay's oration in Richmond, which celebrated Jefferson's presidency and also commented on the Alien and Sedition Laws of the Adams administration.

In Lindsay's words,

> *By the operation of the Alien Law, the legislative and judicial powers were combined and embodied in the Executive. ...The unhappy foreigner who had fled from persecution and proscription in his native realm, whom the torch of hope had lighted to America as the asylum of innocence, who had become naturalized to our constitution and laws, ...now found himself doomed by this iniquitous law to wander an exile on the wide world...*

Lindsay commented on the role of the newspaper in America.

> *Our presses which had hitherto kept alive the spark of seventysix [i.e. 1776] were now stopt — political enquiry was gagged. ...The government of Great Britain, teeming with oppression, boasted not a prouder monument of tyranny than the sedition law.* [28]

Or in the measured view of historian Kevin

Whelan: "the three Alien and Sedition Acts of June and July 1798" were "some of the most repressive legislation ever passed in the United States."[29] (The reader is directed to further discussion of this legislation in the section focusing on Thomas Jefferson.)

Of O'Connor's family life in Norfolk little is known, except that his wife, Elizabeth, died there in 1811 at the age of thirty-seven.

In 1818 the paper included a bit of O'Connor news, the death in County Roscommon (which adjoins County Sligo) of Thomas O'Connor, who was of the ancient line of Roderick O'Connor Don, described as "King of Connaught and Monarch of Ireland."[30] The Norfolk paper published in 1819 a poem written by the celebrated legal defender of the United Irishmen, John Philpot Curran. The occasion was to mark the death of James O'Connor, its editor. The inclusion of the short poem suggests O'Connor's admiration of Curran.[31]

The Green Spot That Blooms
O'er the Desert of Life

O'er the desert of life, where you plainly pursued
Those phantoms of hope which their promise disown,
Have you ne'er met some spirit divinely endued
That so kindly could say, You don't suffer alone?
And however your fate may have smiled or have frown'd,

*Will she deign still to share as the friend or the
wife?
Then make her the pulse of your heart, for
you've found
The green spot that blooms o'er the desert of
life.
Does she love to recall the past moments so
dear,
When the sweet pledge of faith was confidingly
given,
When the lip spoke the voice of affection sin-
cere,
And the vow was exchanged and recorded in
Heaven?
Does she wish to rebind what already was
bound
And draw closer the claim of the friend and the
wife?
Then make her the pulse of your heart, for
you've found
The green spot that blooms o'er the desert of
life.*

Why did James O'Connor come to Norfolk from
Sligo? Let us look briefly at four elements in Ire-
land of the 1780s and 1790s: the Militia Act, the
Defender organization, the press, and the United
Irish movement.

Dramatic things happened in 1793. There were
protest demonstrations and armed actions by the
Defenders all over Ireland. The *casus belli* was the
Militia Act, put into law that year. Its object was
to provide compulsory military service in defense
of the empire. According to Rosamond Jacob, each

Irish county was ordered to enroll five hundred men, and "the officers of this militia were Protestants, while most of the men, of course, were Catholics."[32]

This religio-class distinction meant that natives were considered to be cannon-fodder and expendable. The Act served to politicize local people who reacted with fury at both the compulsory aspect and the anti-nationalist aspect. As Kevin Whelan describes the Defenders: "Their levelling tendencies — 'the cobbler and the Caesar made level' — were derived from an historically based sense of social injustice, applicable to the obvious disparities in eighteenth-century Irish life."[33]

Violent clashes with the military occurred for the next two years. Jim Smyth notes that by March, 1795, "large areas of Cavan, Roscommon, and Sligo were characterized as 'actually in a state of insurrection.'"[34] A Dublin newspaper observed that in June of 1795 "the most atrocious acts [were] committed by soldiery on the poor unoffending peasants."

Smyth comments on the role played in July 1795 by the Earl of Carhampton, Henry Luttrell, who was a Lieutenant General at the time and who later would move savagely against the United insurgents: "Carhampton, in a wholly illegal exercise, had arrested 1300 'Defenders' without charge or trial, and sent them aboard a tender anchored off Sligo, for service in the fleet."[35]

Jacob adds to the picture of events of the day:

In Sligo large bodies of men had assembled under arms to prevent enrollment of their names in the militia, and were said to have committed depredations in the houses of most respectable gentlemen, seizing arms and ammunition and drinking the respectable gentlemen's wines. They were pursued by magistrates with a party of dragoons, and at Ballinafad... there was a sort of battle. The people fired on the dragoons. Nineteen 'insurgents' were killed, and a hundred and twenty-three taken prisoner.[36]

James O'Connor, working in his editor's office on Market Street in Sligo town, would have been aware of the activity swirling about his county in the years before his departure. Since few issues of his *Sligo Morning Herald* have survived, we can only surmise that perhaps he was bold and feckless enough to write about the situation.

The English authorities, after approving the Militia Act passed by their puppet Irish parliament in Dublin, soon came to understand that the occupied country had no liking for it. But after all, were the Irish peasants not grateful for the Catholic Relief Act which became law in 1793? As Thomas Bartlett makes explicit, this relief legislation "was a victory for the Catholic middle classes..., not for the rural poor." That huge sector of the Irish populace soon realized that such relief "had not been accompanied by social reform; it had been accompanied by a Militia Act."[37]

The United Irishmen movement grew during the 1790s. After a few years of organizing and publicizing, it became increasingly repressed by the London authorities and by the puppet regime in Dublin Castle. In the space of a few months, some 30,000 Irish people were killed by the military and its yeomanry supporters. The United movement put a great amount of effort into spreading ideas of equality and democracy among the Irish populace. The United members saw themselves as "bearers of the European Enlightenment, freely importing ideas from England, Scotland, and France."[38] Pamphlets and broadsides and songbooks (*Paddy's Resource* was full of progressive songs) appeared and became well known. The United movement started some newspapers, and other papers were supportive of their efforts.

Whelan describes the growth of journalism and printing: "In the 1790s there was a minimum of fifty printers in Dublin, thirty-four provincial presses..., and at least forty newspapers in print."[39]

Some editors and publishers as early as the 1780s were jailed and fined. In Dublin, newspapers which died included the *Morning Post*, the *Volunteer's Journal*, and the *Press*. In Cork city, the *Harp of Erin* was shut down the same month it began publication. In Belfast, the *Northern Star* endured from 1792 until the military physically destroyed it in a few years.

Financial support was provided by the ruling authorities to Irish papers which supported the government: the *Belfast News-Letter*, *Faulkner's Dublin Journal*, the *Waterford Herald*, and the *Clonmel Herald*.

In Norfolk, James O'Connor no doubt followed the saga of the proprietors and printers of the *Northern Star*. When they went to trial in Dublin their esteemed legal counsel was John Philpot Curran. Despite his brilliant defense in court on their behalf, they were sentenced to one and a half years in prison for sedition. The *Northern Star* had been widely read and was very influential, "and before long it had the largest circulation of any newspaper in Ireland."[40] Small wonder then that the English government despised and feared that newspaper.

Endnotes

1. William S. Forrest, *Historical and Descriptive Sketches of Norfolk and Vicinity* (Philadelphia: Lindsay and Blakiston, 1853), p.115.
2. David Dobson, *Ships From Ireland to Early America 1623–1850* (Baltimore: Genealogical Publishing Co., 1999), *passim*.
3. Dobson, *passim*.
4. Pippenger, index of names.
5. Pippenger, index of names.
6. Forrest, p. 107.
7. Forrest, p. 290.
8. Forrest, pp. 105–6.
9. Forrest, p. 289.
10. Forrest, p 105.
11. Joe McGowan, *Echoes of a Savage Land* (Cork: Mercier Press, 2001), pp. 173–4.
12. Letter of August 14, 2000 in possession of Brian McGinn, sent to Kevin Donleavy.
13. Michael Durey, "The Fate of the Rebels After 1798," in *History Today*, 48 (6) (June 1998), p. 26.
14. *Ulster Journal of Archaelogy*, Vol.13 (August 1907), pp. 104–5.
15. Colonel William H. Stewart, *History of Norfolk, Virginia, and Representative Citizens, 1637–1900* (Chicago: Biographical Publishing, 1902), p. 687.
16. Thomas Packenham, *The Year of Liberty: The History of the Great Irish Rebellion of 1798* (New York: Random House, 1969), p. 282.
17. Stewart, p. 490.
18. William James MacNeven, *Pieces of Irish History: Illustrative of the Condition of the Catholics of Ireland, of the Origin and Progress of the Political System of the United Irishmen, and of their Transactions with the Anglo-Irish Government.*
19. Carl Wittke, *The Irish in America* (Baton Rouge: LSU Press, 1956), p. 76.
20. Rogers Dey Whichard, *The History of Lower Tidewater Virginia*, Vol.1 (New York: Lewis Historical, 1959), p. 467.
21. John Boyle O'Reilly, "Canoeing in the Dismal Swamp," in *Athletics and Manly Sport* (Boston: Pilot Publishing Co., 1888), n.p. (between pp.243–59).
22. O'Reilly, n.p. (between pp. 243–59).
23. Whichard, p. 467.
24. *Norfolk Herald*, July 5, 1819.
25. *Norfolk Herald*, July 5, 1819.

26. *Norfolk Herald*, January 16, 1802.
27. David Dickson, in the Foreword to Richard Musgrave, *Memoirs...*, new edition by Steven W. Myers and Delores E. McKnight (Ft. Wayne: Round Tower Books, 1995), i, xi.
28. *Norfolk Herald*, April 7, 1803.
29. Kevin Whelan, "The Green Atlantic: radical reciprocities between Ireland and America," in Kathleen Wilson, ed., *A New Imperial History — Culture, Identity, and Modernity in Britain and the Empire, 1660–1840* (Cambridge: University Press, 2004), p. 228.
30. *Norfolk Herald*, March 6, 1818.
31. *Norfolk Herald*, July 9, 1819.
32. Rosamond Jacob, *The Rise of the United Irishmen* (London: Harrap, 1937), p. 167.
33. Kevin Whelan, "The United Irishmen, the Enlightenment and Popular Culture," in *The United Irishmen: Republicanism, Radicalism and Rebellion,* ed. David Dickson et al. (Dublin: Lilliput Press, 1993), p. 273.
34. Jim Smyth, *The Men of No Property* (Dublin: Gill and Macmillan, 1992), p. 109.
35. Smyth, p. 110.
36. Jacob, pp. 167–8.
37. Thomas Bartlett, "An End to Moral Economy: The Irish Militia Disturbances of 1793," in *Past and Present*, Vol.99 (May 1983), p. 61.
38. Whelan, in Dickson et al., p. 269.
39. Whelan, in Dickson et al., p. 276.
40. Jacob, p. 178.

CHAPTER 4

Richmond

*H*enrico County was established in 1634, a large geographic area from which ten Virginia counties were eventually formed, as well as the cities of Richmond, Charlottesville, and Colonial Heights. Richmond itself is traditionally assigned the year 1737 as its founding date.

The Master Index of Marriages provides evidence of early Irish presence in the Henrico domain:

Patrick Breney married Anne Gardner in 1782
Michael Ryan married Frances Dudley in 1785
Thomas Donnelly married Jane Douglas in 1787
Mary Donnelly married Hugh Curay in 1787
Peter Mulligan married Kitty Shackleton in 1788
Elizabeth Kelly married William Miller in 1792
Thomas Connor married Jane Jarman in 1792
Michael Shannon married Phebe Kelly in 1793.

There were numerous Murphys in the area who were wed in the late eighteenth and early nineteenth century:

John married Sarah Bryan in 1782
Priscilla married James Boatwright in 1806
Daniel married Jane Woodfin in 1810
Jeremiah married Johanna O'Leary in 1822

Corelius married Mary Bowen in 1829, and in 1818 there was recorded the marriage between Nancy McLaughlin and John McDermott.

There were some fourteen Irish individuals, born in the 1700s, who came to reside in Richmond.

Redmond G. Barry, born in County Cork about 1768, was "for many years a respectable inhabitant of this city;" Barry lived on Third Street, and died in 1843.[1]
Patrick Machen died at "the residence of James Gallagher, on Grace street." Born in 1773, his death occurred in 1844.
A newspaper chronicler tells the reader that "the melancholy duty devolves upon us... of announcing the death" of Patrick Durkin in 1853. Born c.1774, and "one of our oldest and most esteemed citizens," Durkin during his fifty-odd years in the Richmond-Petersburg area served stints as Magistrate, Recorder, and Mayor.
Francis O'Connell lived in Richmond some eighteen years until his death in 1841. He had emigrated from Kerry, his birthplace, in about 1779.
A native of Tyrone, Bernard O'Hagan lived some forty years in Richmond. Born c.1779, his funeral took place in 1853.
Three individuals born in 1781 emigrated to Richmond. Mrs. Mary Collins was born in Dublin and passed away in 1852. Mrs. M. Foagarty died in 1846. And one John Grace

lived until 1841, "a citizen of Richmond for the last 20 years."

Another Kerry native was a Mrs. Elizabeth Harrold, c.1783-1843. She died in Richmond where she had lived "many years."

Mrs. Mary Ann Dornin died in 1852. Her birth occurred in c.1786.

James O'Brien lived at his home called "Aspen Grove" in Henrico County. Born in Cork in about 1788, he died in 1853.

"Long known as a member of the Legislature," John Hooe died in 1842, having been born in Ireland c.1789.

Daniel S. McCarthy was born in Kerry about 1795. He lived some thirty years in Richmond until his death in 1848.

A native of County Carlow where he was born c.1793, a Henry Joice died in 1848 "at his residence, at Holly Mount Cemetery." Perhaps he was a grave-digger.

There were newspaper accounts of the deaths of Irish children in Richmond.

William was a son of Nicholas and Eliza Devereux. John Alexander Sullivan was born to Timothy and Bridget O'Sullivan, who lived near the Tredegar Iron Works. Infant Margaret Ellen's parents were Patrick and Lucy Ellen Fogarty whose home was at the corner of Canal and Second Streets.

Philip and Mary Phelin's son Patrick lived to the age of ten in 1852. Thomas and Martha Daly's son died at age fifteen in that same year. John Dwyer's boy Michael died

very young; the Dwyers lived on Valley Street.
Eleanora McCann's parents were Maurice and Mary. The infant's funeral in 1853 took place at "the residence of her parents, on Oregon Hill."
E.B. Curtin's young son, James P., died in 1853.

Others who lived in Richmond had come from various places in the old country.

There was Francis McKinney, "a native of the county of Monaghan, Ireland, but for many years a respectable inhabitant of this city." His death came in 1853.
Thomas McCormack emigrated from County Monaghan with his brother Michael. They lived on Broad Street; Thomas died at age nineteen in 1853.
Patrick Cavanaugh was a Sligo man. He died in 1845; his wife Mary died in 1843.
Samuel Wheney was a native of County Antrim. His 1845 funeral proceeded "from the house of Mr. Nicholas Ryan, Cary Street."
Thomas W. West came from the County Armagh; he too lived on Cary Street, and died in 1851.
Sylvester Connor was yet another resident of Cary Street; he died in 1852.
A Belfast man was one James Gray. He passed away in 1852.
Michael J. Flood, born c.1822 in Dublin, died in 1851, having spent his last sixteen years

in Richmond.

Rockett's Landing is located near downtown Richmond. It is named "for an Irish immigrant who operated a rope ferry across the James."[2] Robert Rockett began his ferry enterprise on the river in 1730; within a few decades the city was a tremendously busy port. Eventually what came to be called Rockett's Wharf accommodated large steamships until the mid-1800s. In Portlaw, County Waterford, a portion of Rockett's Castle still stands, and can be dated to the year 1212. There were early Rocketts who were born in Virginia: Ware in c.1714, Francis in c.1716, and John in c.1719. Two Rocketts were born in Henrico County: Baldwin in c.1718, and Richard in c.1721.

By the nineteenth century, Irish contributions to Virginia's growth and history become considerably easier to document.

In the early 1800s, one James Connelly was a well-known builder in Richmond.[3]

A mayor of the city was Carleton McCarthy, born there in 1847. His father was a native of Ireland; his mother was born in the U.S. A prominent city attorney was James Lyons, a grandson of Judge Peter Lyons. James built a house called "Laburnum" in the city; it burned in 1864.

Captain Page McCarty started the *Richmond Times* in 1886 and became its editor. Dr. Hunter H. McGuire, 1835-1900, became the physician to Gen. Stonewall Jackson. McGuire taught surgery at the Medical College of Virginia; his summer home in the city was known as "Westwood." (See also the Winchester chapter.)

Hollywood Cemetery in the city is the resting-place of many of Irish extraction, including McGuire. Others include William Burke, born in Ireland in 1821, who died in 1852. He was the master at a boys' school at Eleventh and Marshall Streets; one pupil was the writer Edgar Allan Poe.

Joseph Reid Anderson (1813-1892) was of Irish descent. In 1848 he became owner of Tredegar Iron Works. He became a brigadier general in the Confederate forces; he is interred at Hollywood. He is to be admired for his educated and humane views: not a racist, he saw to it that equal wages at Tredegar be paid to blacks and whites.

Charles T. O'Ferrall (1840 to 1905) entertained black guests at the Governor's Mansion in Richmond during his term of office as the state's chief executive, and he used the state militia to prevent lynchings of black citizens. He is buried at Hollywood.

The immense Iron Works were situated on the James River in the heart of the city. Many Irish worked there, and many worked on the Canal which begins in Richmond.

A "Notice to Contractors" appeared in the city newspaper in 1838:

> *Proposals will be accepted upon the 19th of May next for the construction of all the Farm Bridges on the 30 miles of the James River and Kanawha Canal, between Richmond and Maiden's*

Adventure.[4]

On May 5 the following notice appeared in the newspaper:

> *The James River and Kanawha Canal Company are in immediate want of several hundred Labourers, to work on the said Canal, within three miles of the City of Richmond. For good labourers, one dollar per day will be paid, they finding their own board. Gentlemen wishing to send Negroes from the country, are assured that the very best care shall be taken of them. The work is dry, and I believe perfectly safe. The board of Negroes shall only cost one dollar per week...*
>
> — *Richard Reins, Agent of the JR & K Company*

The celebrated French-born engineer, Claudius Crozet, surveyed land for the canal, and in the 1824 volume of the Board of Public Works Field Notes he briefly alludes to "St. Patrick's Rocks" and "the Irish Falls" in the Blue Ridge Mountains.

In 1835, St. Peter's Catholic Church was built at the corner of Grace and Eighth Streets. It served the many Irish who came to help build the canal and, later, the railroad. The Montgomery Guards was the name of a rifle company recruited from St. Peter's parish in 1861; its captain was John Dooley. (From the 1830s on, there was another militia known as the Hibernian Guard.)

Among the most prominent of Richmonders

in its history have been the Dooley family. John Dooley emigrated from Limerick in the 1830s, and within twenty years he "rose from clerking in various mercantile establishments to operating his own business."[5] Before the Famine, there were some 500 Irish-born in the city; by 1860, some 2200 were living there. Dooley and his wife Sarah became active financial supporters of civic organizations, such as St. Joseph's Orphanage. Their son James, an attorney, served in the legislature in the 1870s. He did well with business investments, particularly the railroads, and he and his wife Sallie bequeathed their home, "Maymont," along with one hundred acres to the city as a park and a museum. These Dooleys built "Swannanoa" on Afton Mountain as a summer home. A palace of white marble in a grand Italian Renaissance style on 120 acres, it is today a stunning edifice.

Readers curious about the city should spend some time with Marie Tyler-McGraw's book, *At the Falls: Richmond, Virginia, and Its People.*[6] Her comments on neighborhood ethnography, racial relations, and the role of labor organizing are very useful. Here are some pertinent passages:

> The late antebellum era saw significant immigration into the city from Ireland and Germany, more hired-out slaves, new homes and factories, and an uneasy jostling for place among the many groups and individuals who made up the growing city. This striving for position was apparent in strikes of white labor against

the introduction of black labor. (112)

German and Irish immigrants clustered first in industrial neighborhoods, often living next to free blacks and boarding-out slaves. (114)

City politics in the 1880s and 1890s featured an important alliance between James Bahen, an Irish immigrant grocer and saloon keeper in Jackson Ward, and John Mitchell, editor of the city's black newspaper, the Richmond Planet. (199)

Ms. Tyler-McGraw points out that there were concentrations of Irish people living in the urban areas known as Fulton, Oregon Hill, and Jackson wards.

In 1885, Terence Powderly visited the city. He was national head of the Knights of Labor, a very progressive and conscientious national union which included among its members unskilled workers, women, and black people. It is significant that Powderly arranged that the Knights hold their 1886 national convention in Richmond.

Among the mighty battles waged in Ireland during the 1800s was the Land War. The aim was to restore ownership of the land to the people of Ireland, and this movement begun by Michael Davitt and Charles Stewart Parnell — the Land League — came into being in 1879. Substantial financial backing came from immense numbers of Irish supporters across the breadth of the United States.

In Richmond there was a sizable branch of the

Irish National Land League during the 1880s. John Murphy was the chairman; among the Board members were James T. Ferriter, J.V. Reddy, William Rankin, Timothy Kerse, James L. Capston, and E.P. Murphy.

Part of the membership proposal of the branch to prospective members reads as follows:

> *The Platform of the Irish National League is one upon which all reasonable men of Irish blood can honestly stand together. The sympathy of our American countrymen we earnestly invite for the just claims of a country whose people in America and Ireland have been, from earliest dawn of Rebellion in the American Colonies to the latest hour of American Independence, their staunch and stalwart allies.*[7]

The size of the city's Irish-American sector is reflected in the plenitude of Irish music in nineteenth-century Richmond.

In 1822, a Mrs. Sully sang Irish songs at a city concert, including "As Down By Banna's Banks I Strayed." The following year, a Mr. Keane sang "Cushlamachree, or Dear Erin." A Miss Gillingham sang "Kate Kearney" in 1827, and Mrs. Morley sang "Young Rory O'Moore" in 1837.

In 1839, a Madame O'Connor, accompanying herself (on piano? on harp?) sang in Gaelic, "Savourneen ma Dellish." Mr. Dempster in 1845 sang the "Lament of an Irish Emigrant," which he had composed. There was a violinist, one Joseph

Burke, who performed at an 1850 concert.

Noted banjo player Joe Sweeney played tunes on an instrument that he had made (1836). In 1864, one F.N. Crouch sang "Black-Eyed Susan" and "Oh, Molly Bawn."

There are two fascinating musical incidents cited in the *Richmond Commercial Compiler*. In its edition of April 21, 1819, we read of a Patrick Connelly who gave a "concert of music, comprising the Irish Bag-Pipes and Violin." A few years later, we learn of a musician called Denny (his surname). This "celebrated performer on the Pipes" was to give "a concert on the Violin and Patent Union Pipes at the Union Hotel." Furthermore, "He will perform on both instruments...a number of Scotch and Irish Airs, & c. together with some fashionable Waltzes."[8]

Another indicator of the Irishness of Richmond is the reception accorded over the years to six noteworthy visitors from Ireland: John Daly Burk in 1801, Tom Moore (1803), Harman Blennerhasset (1807), Thomas Meagher (1853), John Mitchel (1854 and 1855), and Eamon de Valera in 1919.

Born about 1772, Burk was expelled from Trinity College, Dublin, for his political beliefs. He joined the United Irishmen, and shortly thereafter was forced to flee to America. He was a playwright and newspaper editor in Boston, New York, Richmond, and ultimately Petersburg where he was killed in an 1808 duel. His formal, semi-state funeral was marked by "a very large procession, including the artillery, cavalry, and infantry companies of the town."⁹

Burk authored a study of the 1798 insurrection in Ireland, as well as a *History Of Virginia* in several volumes. For the latter work, Thomas Jefferson himself lent Burk research materials from his own library.

The Daughters of the American Revolution has erected a cenotaph to Burk in the Old Blandford Cemetery in Petersburg.

Another United Irishman exile in Petersburg, John McCreery, collaborated with Burk to produce *A Selection, From The Ancient Music Of Ireland, Arranged For The Flute Or Violin.* Published in 1824, it includes poems written by both Burk and McCreery.

It seems safe to assert that this was the first appearance in print of this music in Virginia. There were such songs as "Crushkeen Lawn," "O'Rourk's Feast," "O'Donnel: or, the Hawk of Ballyshannon," and "Kitty Tyrell." There were some pieces by the renowned harper, O'Carolan: "John Nugent," "Planxty Connor," "Mrs. Waller," "Planxty M'Guire," and "Carolan's Receipt." Dance tunes notated were such jigs as "Paddy O'Carrol," and reels such as "Jackson's Chickens." A very unusual tune was "The Rolling Pin," a jig in six parts.

Included in this publication was an essay on Irish music, probably written by Dr. Thomas Robinson. He was another United exile, and a friend of Robert Emmet and Tom Moore at Trinity College. Robinson met with Moore in Norfolk on the latter's 1803-1804 trip to the eastern United States (see also the Norfolk chapter).

The United Irishmen were initially aiming for political reform in Ireland. As the organization was increasingly and brutally repressed, they began to prepare for an armed struggle against England for an independent Irish republic. The English military crushed this republican effort, leaving 30,000 Irish dead, principally in the counties of Antrim, Wexford, and Mayo.

Thomas Jefferson and other innumerable American republicans gained much support from these Irish republicans, these United men, who fled to the US. Jefferson himself wrote a letter of recommendation for Robinson to James Monroe:

> *Mr. Robinson proposing to go to*
> *Richmond with a view to establish*
> *an academy there, I have been*
> *desired to State you his character*
> *and qualifications.... He is a United*
> *Irishman and therefore was obliged to*
> *leave Ireland. He is of course a good*
> *Republican.*[10]

Tom Moore is well known for his many songs, the *Irish Melodies*, the first volume of which was published in 1807. As Linda Kelly observes, "For Irish emigrants throughout the nineteenth century, they were the closest imaginative link with their homeland."[11]

Moore, during his Trinity College days, held back from committing fully to the UI liberation movement of the 1790s. But the 1798 Rising came close to his heart:

Its effects on him were long lasting, leaving him on the one hand with a horror of violence and bloodshed, on the other with a commitment to the seemingly hopeless cause of Irish liberty.[12]

The execution by hanging and beheading (1803) of his good friend Emmet shook him deeply, as one realizes in reading the words in his song for Emmet, "Oh! Breathe not his Name."

Moore visited eastern America for a year, arriving in 1803 only a few months after Emmet's hanging. He spent time in Norfolk, Richmond, Washington, Baltimore, Philadelphia, and New York, as well as Canada. He was well received everywhere:

In 1803 came Tom Moore, Irish poet, "whose songs were sung to every guitar and harpsichord in Richmond."[13]

Moore conquered Philadelphia: here there was an established society, one of the redoubts of the old regime, and it took Moore to its hospitable bosom.[14]

Thomas Jefferson's granddaughter gave him a copy of Moore's *Melodies* when it first appeared in print. As Jefferson was reading in it, he remarked, "Why, this is the little man who satirised me so!"[15]

Moore had written a telling quatrain a short time after he had been introduced to Jefferson:

The patriot, fresh from Freedom's councils come, Now pleased retires to lash his slaves at home; Or woo perhaps some black Aspasia's charms,

And dream of freedom in his bondsmaid's arms.[16]

The aged Jefferson was so moved by Moore's songs that he mentioned the following lines in a farewell letter to his daughter:

It is not the tear at this moment shed,
When the cold turf has just been laid o'er him,
That can tell how beloved was the soul that's fled
Or how deep in our hearts we deplore him.

Although Moore outlived his revolutionary friends and became, in a sense, the musical darling of English and Anglo-Irish society, he maintained his principled outlook on life:

I verily believe...that being born a slave
has but given me a keener sense and
relish of the inestimable blessings of
freedom, and an enlarged sense of
sympathy with all those — whatever their
race or creed, whether they be blacks or
whites — who even with a glimmering
sense of what they seek, are contending
for those just rights and privileges of
civilised man, without which civilisation
itself, in its truest sense, can not exist.[17]

Our third Irish visitor to Richmond received a grim and unfriendly reception. Harman Blennerhasset, another United Irishman exile, was incarcerated in 1807 because of his participation in Aaron Burr's Mexican scheme. Fortunately, Blennerhasset had his flute with him to help while away the hours in jail.[18]

Thomas Francis Meagher was a powerful leader of the 1848 Rising in Ireland. "Meagher of the Sword," as he was called, was transported by the English government to Van Dieman's Land, but managed to escape and come on a fund-raising and educational tour of the United States. In 1853 he spoke in Richmond at the First African Baptist Church. He "expounded on the myriad ties binding Ireland and America together. At the top of his list was a warm reverence for American republicanism, the aspiration of his own country."[19]

Meagher was a good friend of John Mitchel, another articulate and able prisoner in Van Dieman's Land to which he too had been exiled in 1848. In America he published his book, *Jail Journal, Or Five Years In British Prisons*. Mitchel came to Richmond first in 1854, and then again in 1855. During the Civil War, he was editor of the *Richmond Enquirer*, and was jailed in the city in 1865 for his pro-slavery efforts and activities with the Confederate forces.

In 1919, at the height of the Irish war for independence, Eamon de Valera, the new President of the new Irish Republic, did a fundraising tour of American cities. The English military had executed sixteen of the Irish Rising leaders in 1916, sparing de Valera because of his American birth. In New York, de Valera was well received by huge Irish-American audiences.

He came to speak in Richmond in August, 1919, at the urging of a prominent attorney, Daniel C.

O'Flaherty. Daniel had been born in the Shenandoah Valley, but his father — also Daniel — had come to the US in 1850, fleeing the horrors of An Gorta Mor, the huge Famine. The younger O'Flaherty had begun his law practice in Front Royal, where he built a large frame house which he called "Aughnanure," thus naming it after the "ancestral castle of the O'Flahertys of Galway."[20]

De Valera, president of the new Irish government, first spoke in the House of Delegates, "whose members stood to receive him." But the commentary from the *Richmond Times-Dispatch* is poignant:

> *In silence the Virginia Assembly listened as the tall representative of Ireland told it that his country was asking for the same thing for which Washington fought, Jefferson wrote, and [Patrick] Henry made his impassioned plea. Neither by word nor token did any of its members give assent to his argument.[21]*

Later the same day, de Valera spoke in the city auditorium to some 3500 listeners. During his talk, "the audience provided almost continuous applause."[22]

The contrast in de Valera's reception was very strong. The bulk of the legislature's members, for the most part, thought of themselves as ruling-class Anglophiles. The auditorium crowd, on the other hand, were understanding of and sympathetic toward the Irish struggle.

Endnotes

1. Wesley E. Pippenger, ed., *Death Notices from Richmond, Virginia Newspapers 1841–1853* (Richmond, VA: Virginia Genealogical Society, 2002).
2. *AIArchitect*, Volume 14 (October 5, 2007).
3. Letter, Charles Ellis to John H. Cocke, 19 June 1816, in *Cocke Papers*, Special Collections, University of Virginia Library, Charlottesville.
4. *Richmond Whig and Public Advertiser*, May 1 and May 5, 1838.
5. Norman C. McLeod, "'Not Forgetting the Land We Left': The Irish in Antebellum Richmond," in *Virginia Cavalcade*, Winter 1998, p.37.
6. Marie Tyler-McGraw, *At the Falls: Richmond, Virginia, and Its People*. Chapel Hill, NC: University of North Carolina Press, 1994.
7. *Broadside* 188-I68, Box c.2, Special Collections, Library of Virginia, Richmond.
8. Albert L. Stoutamire, *A History of Music in Richmond Virginia From 1742 to 1865*. Dissertation, Florida State University, 1960, pp.116–7.
9. Edward A. Wyatt, IV, *John Daly Burk: Patriot-Playwright-Historian* (Charlottesville, VA: The Historical Publishing Co., 1936), p.26.
10. Letter, Thomas Jefferson to James Monroe, 16 February 1800, at http://wiki.monticello.org/mediawiki/index.php/Ireland.
11. Linda Kelly, *Ireland's Minstrel—A Life of Tom Moore* (London: Tanris, 2006), p.1.
12. Kelly, *Ireland's Minstrel—A Life of Tom Moore*, p. 31.
13. Terence de Vere White, *Tom Moore the Irish Poet* (London: Hamish Hamilton, 1977), p.48.
14. White, *Tom Moore the Irish Poet*, p. 48.
15. White, *Tom Moore the Irish Poet*, p.47.
16. White, *Tom Moore the Irish Poet*, p.47.
17. Kelly, *Ireland's Minstrel — A Life of Tom Moore*, p.2.
18. David A. Wilson, *United Irishmen, United States: Immigrant Radicals in the Early Republic* (Ithaca, NY: Cornell University Press, 1998), p.160.
19. McLeod, "'Not Forgetting the Land We Left': The Irish in Antebellum Richmond," in *Virginia Cavalcade*, Winter 1998, p.44.
20. James C. O'Flaherty, "Daniel C. O'Flaherty, 1862-1929: Ireland's Good Friend," in *Virginia Cavalcade*, Autumn 2002, p.150.
21. O'Flaherty, "Daniel C. O'Flaherty, 1862-1929: Ireland's Good Friend," in *Virginia Cavalcade*, Autumn 2002, p.151.
22. O'Flaherty, "Daniel C. O'Flaherty, 1862-1929: Ireland's Good

Friend," in *Virginia Cavalcade*, Autumn 2002, p.152.

CHAPTER 5

Other Locales

𝔗his chapter deals with some of the one hundred or so locales and communities in Virginia that have had an Irish presence, great or small, since the 1600s. Once these immigrants arrived "across the western ocean," they made their way in every direction. In some cases, printed sources document the Irishness; in others, little is known other than a place-name itself. Most of these sites can be found on present-day maps and gazetteers.

Fairfax County and Alexandria have had a sizable number of Irish-born citizens. Between 1742 and 1853, the following individuals found spouses in the Fairfax jurisdiction:

Patrick Callaghan	*Nancy Kicheloe*
Mary Conner	*Margaret Conner*
Elizabeth Keane	*Elizabeth Connell*
Sarah Kincheloe	*Ellen M. Burke*
John W. Lynch	*Lynna Ann Reardon*
Elizabeth Kincheloe	*Michael O'Meara*

Applications submitted by Irish immigrants for citizenship in Fairfax were numerous: some seventy-four, from 1820 through the 1850s. Patrick Thomas Renney, born in Ireland, applied in 1824. William Morgan, John Burke, Frances Marie Tracey, Bernard Drury, and William Kehoe made application before the onset of Ireland's famine in the 1840s. The remainder appear to have emigrated to escape the Famine and English neglect, as they applied in the 1840s.[2] In the mid-1800s, the first Fairfax railroad station was built by Irish immigrants, and many of them worked to construct the rail lines. They also helped build St. Mary's Church, where many Irish are buried, both Union and Confederate soldiers.

There is a historical marker on Huntsman Boulevard entering Shannon Station. It marks the location of Keene's Mill, which was located on Pohick Creek. James Keene built his mill some time after 1796.

The town of Alexandria was the Fairfax county seat in the middle to late 1700s. Tax and census records help to fill in an early Irish era in the town. Thomas Fitzpatrick built a house on the 500 block of Duke Street in the late 1700s, and one Alex McConnell had a Duke Street house for rent in the 1790s.

Michael Madden built a three-bay, three-story house circa 1786 on Prince Street. James McGuire owned land on Prince Street when houses were built there in 1816-1818. McGuire also built on Queen Street, and this "house joiner" also constructed three brick houses on North Royal Street.

On South Royal, Edward McLaughlin in 1832 deeded his house to a daughter, Bridget. At 509 South Lee Street, a two-story, three-bay brick house was built in 1811-12 by Captain John McNamara. The well-known Colonel John Fitzgerald (more of him later) lived on South Lee, and owned warehouses on King Street. And one James McVeigh put up a house circa 1850 on Cameron Street.

Thanks to the archival death reports collected by Wesley Pippenger, we can trace more immigrants in the Alexandria area. The following men and women were born in Ireland in the 1700s:

> *Mr John Lourdan, a promising young gentleman, a native of Ireland, died here* [in 1785] *deservedly regretted by his Acquaintance. His Death was occasioned by a Mortification of one of his legs, which he broke, a few Days ago, in riding an unruly Horse.*[3]

In 1815 Captain John McClenachan died at age sixty in neighboring Prince William County: "Few men possessed more social and benevolent virtues."[4]

Richard Walsh died at the age of thirty-nine in 1815. Matthew Gorman died in 1819, Richard McDonnell in 1820, and Mrs. Mary Nicholson in 1821 at age eighty.

Patrick Burns, "native of Ireland," died in 1820 at "his residence on the toll-gate of the Alexandria & Washington turnpike."[5] James Kiernan, eulogized as "an affectionate husband and tender father," passed away in 1823 at age twenty-six. He was born at Coragh in the County Cavan.[6]

> *On the decease of Thomas Irwin (1827, age 65), Alexandria lost one of the oldest and most intelligent merchants of this place. He was gifted by nature with a clear and vigorous mind, improved by close observation, and disciplined by long*

experience.[7]

In 1828, death came to Patrick Laphen at age 45, "after a short but painful illness, which he bore with Christian fortitude and resignation."[8]

James Francis Tracy had "lived to a good old age" when he passed away "at Mount Erin, the seat of his residence, near this place" (i.e., near Alexandria). James had been "known, by many of the most respectable families in Md. and Va., as a teacher of music, and a scholar." He was a Dublin man.[9]

At his death at age 92 in 1834, the obituary for Daniel McCormick was headed, "A Patriarch Gone." His eulogist continued, "This worthy man...settled in this city long prior to the Revolution," and had been "a merchant of great probity and honor."[10]

Old Point Comfort was the locale of the final days of Thomas M. Fitzgerald, noted as a "professor of dancing" in Alexandria. He died in 1834. The following year Robert Sands died at age forty-three.[11]

Born about 1746, Matthew Gorman died in Alexandria in 1819; he had moved to the city from Boston.

The first Catholic church in Alexandria was built in 1795; the present church went up in 1826. The first church was sited on land that is now part of the old Catholic cemetery, at Church and South Washington Streets.

"Colonel John Fitzgerald is the most prominent Irishman remembered in Alexandria." Historian Brian McGann, never prone to exaggeration, voiced this overview of the Irish-born man who became the loyal and capable aide-de-camp to General George Washington during the Revolutionary War.[12]

Fitzgerald had emigrated and arrived in Alexandria about 1770, soon met Washington, and was constantly at his side. Fitzgerald served as mayor of the town in 1786—87, and he and Washington became partners in commerce: directors of the Potomac Company, canal-building on that river. Most of the physical labor at the canals was performed by Irish immigrants.

Fitzgerald's death in 1799 was marked by an immense and impressive solemnity. The funeral procession, from his residence through the streets of the town, consisted of the following elements:

> *A company of Light Infantry.*
> *Music.*
> *Two companies of Infantry.*
> *Guards.*
> *A company of Riflemen.*
> *Mourning Relatives.*
> *A company of Artillery.*
> *Corpse.*
> *Militia Officers.*
> *Pall Bearers.*[13]

At the time of Fitzgerald's death, some three hundred Irish indentured servants had settled in Alexandria.

Nearby Westmoreland County has early Irish links. Kinsale was known as a deep-water port on the Potomac as early as 1706. It became a registered town in 1784, and apparently there had been a post office established there by the 1790s.

The Yeocomico River had a number of Irish affiliations. Lynch's Point, on the north side of the river, derived its name from Francis Lynch, who was the land-owner circa 1706. Shannon Branch is the northern fork of the Yeocomico.

An early and very prominent citizen of Westmoreland County was Dennis McCarty, who in 1677 married one Elizabeth Billington. Their son, Daniel ,(born 1684) came to marry Elizabeth Payne, and another son, Dennis, in 1724 married Sarah Ball, kin to George Washington's family.

Daniel owned land in Richmond and Westmoreland counties. In 1707 he served as King's Attorney concerning an estate of Colonel John Washington. Daniel found time to serve Westmoreland in the state House of Burgesses, and was Speaker of the House in 1715-18. He is interred at Yeocomico Church; his monument indicates that his death occurred in 1724 when he was forty-nine years of age.

Others in this McCarty clan were landowners in Stafford, Northumberland, and Rappahannock counties. (Readers interested in the early McCarty matter can consult the *William and Mary Quarterly*.[14])

Hogan's Hill in Westmoreland is named for Richard J. Hogan, who owned land there during the 1800s. The local name "Irish Neck," which has not been used since about 1850, refers to an upper corner of the county, at the confluence of Rozier Creek and the Potomac River.

The early communities in eastern Virginia were aided in their growth by sailing ships bringing transatlantic passengers up the larger rivers. There are interesting incidents attached to some of these voyages of the eighteenth century.

In 1792, an Englishman, John Cunningham, was master of a brigantine (two main masts) bearing his name. An ill-fated voyage: "Bound from Ireland to America with Emigrants, [it] was captured off the Capes of Virginia by a French Privateer, called the Sans Cullotis, of Marseilles, sometime September last, and carried to Baltimore."[15]

Extreme weather in the Atlantic ports often greeted incoming travelers, as with this unnamed ship in 1747:

> *...an immigrant vessel in route from Ireland to Fredericksburg foundered while entering the mouth of the Rappahannock River. Quickly capsized by the tropical cyclone's roaring seas, the ship carried more than 50 people to the bottom with it, many of them indentured servants.[16]*

This incident occurred in the broad expanse of river (some five fathoms in depth) at Urbanna, a community large enough to have had a prison in the 1770s.

A full description, with ironic commentary, of a 1773 incident at the mouth of the York River appeared in the *Maryland Gazette*. An unnamed brig sailing out of Dublin carried some 150 "indentured servants and convict laborers":

> *...she carried a crew of seventeen and a*

*captain destined never to see dry land
again. ...In January, when the vessel
reached the tidewater, she was entirely
under the control of [the passengers],
none of whom had any intentions
of spending their time sentences in
servitude. When a pilot boat put out...to
guide the ship in, she was immediately
seized by thirty convicts. The boat was
run ashore and the convicts escaped.
The remainder of their compatriots...
had little alternative but to try to run
their own vessel ashore and escape
the best way they could... But the
escapees had apparently prepared well
for their flight, probably to the western
frontier of Virginia. By January 21 only
four men and a single woman were
retaken. ...What is certain, however, is
that perhaps as many as one hundred
individuals eluded the fate of bondage.
Freedom, deserved or not, was theirs.
The same freedom that their would-be
masters soon fought a revolution for.[17]*

(The attentive reader may recall the discussion of indentureship in the chapter entitled, "Early Irish: Servants? Slaves?")

Judicial records of Westmoreland County suggest that life in the late seventeenth century had its intensities, including marital conflicts. In the 1672-73 court session, the following was recorded:

*Dorothy Veale called Mrs. Elenor Quigley
Irish whore and Irish bitch and Irish
witch and Irish hagg and Irish baud. Mrs.*

> *Veale then warned the Irish woman that*
> *if I had you heere I would stampe you*
> *under my feete.*[18]

In Northumberland County, among the early settlers was one Charles Fallon, probably born in Ireland, whose land purchase was put on record in 1671.

Some Sweeneys arrived in Virginia in the mid-seventeenth century. Of them, the historian/archivist John Boddie writes:

> *Edmund Sweeney, first of his family*
> *in Virginia, is said to have been born*
> *in Ireland. He and his family were*
> *headrights of Mr. Thomas Purefoy who*
> *patented two thousand acres on the*
> *south side of the Rappahannock River,*
> *Mar. 13, 1655 for the transportation of*
> *40 persons.*[19]

The Sweeneys rose to prominence in Elizabeth City County. Edmund was a Justice in the county court in 1692; he died about 1697.

Among the Irish immigrants who were landed up the Rappahannock River in communities such as Fredericksburg and Tappahannock were some skilled wood-workers and furniture makers. (Readers are referred to an article by Ronald Hurst, "Irish Influences on Cabinetmaking in Virginia's Rappahannock River Basin.")[20] By 1775, Fredericksburg had a population of some 1500, and Tappahannock (in Essex County) numbered only a few hundred souls. Richmond County (not the city of that name) borders these counties. In the parish of

Lunenburg in the late 1700s, James Kelly had as taxables twelve white people and thirteen blacks. Daniel Connollee had four whites, John Kelly had eleven whites and nine blacks, and Gerrard McKenny had four white, three black.[21]

A portrait of Judge Peter Lyons by the celebrated painter Thomas Sully now hangs in the Virginia Supreme Court Building. Born in County Cork in 1734, Lyons graduated from Trinity College, Dublin. He was elected a Virginia Supreme Court judge in 1788; his death occurred at Studley Plantation (where Patrick Henry was born) in Hanover County in 1809.

Another nearby county is Stafford, in which a small Irish presence can be spotted. The southern border of this county is the Rappahannock River; on the east, the county is defined by the Potomac.

Among the eighteenth-century landowners in Stafford are:

John Kelly, with 50 acres in 1704
William Kelly, 50 acres in 1704
Cornelius Keefe, 890 acres in 1714-15
Edward Ryley, 600 acres in 1715
John McGuire, 625 acres in 1726 and 1731
Bryan O'Bannion, 635 acres in 1728
Michael Regan, 179 acres in 1729
Alex McCarty, 830 acres in 1729-30[22]

Surnames in Overwharton parish in Stafford include the following newlyweds: Cassity, Connally, Costello, Dillon, Doyle, Foley, Hayes, Mac-

Cartee, McGuirk, O'Bannion, and O'Cane. Among the parish deaths are Mary Murphy's in 1741, Edward Cavenaugh's in 1742, and William McCarty's in 1743.

An interesting character is one John Mercer, born in Dublin town, who emigrated to Stafford in 1726. He married Catherine Mason, "and thus at the tender age of twenty-one Mercer became a member of Virginia's aristocracy." In point of fact, "Within just fifteen years of his arrival in the New World, Mercer had established himself as an able planter, superb administrator, and brilliant lawyer."[23]

There was a William Irvine who at the age of eighty-four owned some 5,000 acres in Stafford, on which he employed his 125 slaves. He and his wife, Sarah, built their own place and named it Hartwood House, which is still standing today. Of William, we are told that he "left his native Ireland in 1803 to escape religious persecution," he being a Presbyterian.[24]

Stafford was politically divided in its early era, as was much of the new white-man's world. Tories and Whigs went at it tooth and nail.

A local Whig reactionary was John Waugh. A modern commentator, Eby, notes that in the 1680s, "wild accusations" came forth from Waugh, who was a parson. He "enraged local farmers by preaching that Maryland Catholics were conspiring with the Seneca Indians... to murder the Protestants in Stafford."

Eby continues: "Armed and vengeful, Waugh's

band headed for Woodstock with plans to kill Brent and burn his property." (George Brent was a Catholic in Stafford.) Ultimately Waugh and his co-conspirators were arrested, and Waugh himself was made to apologize publicly.[25]

The reverend Mr. Waugh was atypical, Eby assures us. In the pre-Revolutionary age, the Stafford area "actually welcomed people of varying beliefs."[26]

The thoughtful reader may ponder the religious demagoguery and deadly hatred in Ireland, which was directed toward native Irish people from the seventeenth century on by the newly-arrived Scots and English usurpers.

Loudoun County saw an early group of settlers in 1732 in what came to be named Milltown. Thomas Moore, a local cobbler, re-named it Waterford, its present-day name, "in memory of his birthplace in Waterford, Ireland."[27]

Two houses in Hanover County had names connected to Ireland: "Emmett," which was owned by one Terrell, and "Sligo," owned by a Redd. Perhaps Terrell was a somewhat influential local, since the first paved road in Hanover county stretched "from Beaver Dam south to C.T. Terrell's store."[28]

In the Shenandoah Valley, it is said that McGaheysville "was settled in the late eighteenth century by a group of Irishmen." A settler born in Dover, Delaware, but of Irish lineage, moved to Virginia and became the first postmaster of this community in 1801; with "typical Irish modesty, he named the town after himself."[29] (He was probably Tobias or

William McGahey.)

There are a few Irish items pertaining to Orange County. Ballintobber Farm was named in the 1940s by Dr. and Mrs. Henry Bonynge, in memory of a much older Bonynge property in Ireland.[30] Orange County seems to have hosted one Philemon Cananaugh or Kavanaugh, who died about 1742 or so; he was born in Ireland. There was also another Philemon Kavanaugh junior who lived in neighboring Culpeper County; born in Ireland's County Cavan in either 1711 or 1737, he died in 1764. This second man was said to be the son of a Philemon senior, whose life stretched from 1669 to 1743.

Montpelier, the mansion and estate of President James Madison, is a monument to the eighteenth century. After the death of the president and his wife Dolly, the property was sold to Thomas J. Carson, born in Ireland, who after emigrating had become a prominent banker in Baltimore. He and an eccentric brother Frank lived at Montpelier from 1857 to 1881. Frank died at age sixty-two in 1881 and is buried close by the presidential couple in Montpelier graveyard.

The Murphy community in Buchanan County is called after the first postmaster, a Richard Murphy, who also served as a local Justice of the Peace.[31]

There was one Colonel Samuel Dabney Burke, whose name is memorialized at Burkeville in Nottoway County. He apparently lived from 1794 to 1880.[32]

A family is commemorated in Rileyville in Page County; the town got its name in the year 1885.[33]

Several places in southwestern Virginia demonstrate Irish connections.

William Christian (c.1743-86) is identified on the website Wikipedia as "a soldier and politician for Virginia." His family shifted from the Isle of Man to Ireland, then emigrated to Virginia in 1740 and built a general store. Christiansburg is named for William, who is also given credit for naming the settlement of Dublin in Pulaski County.[34]

Another archivist, Darst, refers to Dublin as New Dublin, "a trading post likely established by a Dublin Irishman." Darst adds that New Dublin Presbyterian Church was organized by 1769, and by 1779 "James McCorkle operated a store there." The citation adds intriguing details:

> *The accounts of McCorkle's store...*
> *reveal what wagons brought to the*
> *trading center: cotton, linen and silk*
> *yard goods; threads, needles, ribbons,*
> *lace; felt and raccoon hats and hatboxes*
> *for gentlemen; shirts, stockings, looking*
> *glasses, watch chains, silk bonnets,*
> *pewter tableware, frying pans, guns,*
> *knives, saddles, stirrups, clawhammers,*
> *writing paper, books, medicine; and*
> *innumerable other items.[35]*

And there is a Little Irish Mountain within the bounds of Pulaski County.

As for the Keen Mountain located in Buchanan County, "many families have Keen as a family name," according to Raus Hanson. She also reminds the reader that the crossroads spot bearing the name Keene in Albemarle County "was named for a man who married into the Randolph family."[36] (See also the Charlottesville and Lynchburg chapters.)

The Clinch River, famed in song and legend, flows through Russell and Scott counties. Hanson provides us with this anecdote:

> *It takes its name from the hunter who found it. Another report regarding the river name is that an Irishman fell from a raft and called "Clinch me! Clinch me!"*[37]

The Quillin house in Scott County is comprised of two log cabins, each two stories in height. A Federal-style house was built on top of the logs sometime between 1790 and 1830. It appears to be the oldest house in the county.

Enumerated in the 1820 census were James, John, and William Quillin, all having sons in their respective families. The homestead was Quillinsville, now known as Snowflake, in the vicinity of the Hiltons area. (Note also the Quillen Ridge located in Grayson County.)

Among the few communities nearby are McConnell and Dungannon, and there is another McConnell in Russell County, just east of Abingdon. (Russell also has the Bangor and Belfast Mills communities.)

Captain Patrick Hagan (1828-1917) gave the name Dungannon in Scott County for his homeplace in Ireland, and there is a lengthy Virginia newspaper article about his life and career.[38] His uncle, Joseph Hagan, acquired more than 300,000 acres in the area during the 1830s and 1840s, and a Bernard Hagan of Richmond was an attorney for some of the land transactions. (Probably the Bernard, 1779-1853, who emigrated from County Tyrone and was a Richmond resident from about 1813.)

Patrick came to the U.S. in 1844, and soon inherited some of his uncle's land. In 1860 he built a lovely residence of timber, calling it Hagan House, at Sulphur Spring, a few miles from Dungannon. The newspaper notes that "Hagan House had steam heat, two or more bathrooms...for that day of rustic living."[39] This prominent Irish man developed a thriving law practice, and his investments in mining and timber brought him considerable wealth.

And the town of Dungannon back in County Tyrone was becoming a place of tense pre-revolutionary activity. In the 1780s, members of the large Volunteer corps gathered at the Dungannon parish church "and pledged their support to resolutions in favour of legislative independence." In the following decade, a number of political thinkers and reformers met in Dungannon, "the delegates pledging their support to parliamentary reform."[40] It is reasonable to assume that the older Hagans, Joseph and Bernard, could sense the coming storm, that the English ruling class would unleash its military on such thinkers and reformers.

Campbell County has a small community called Gladys, but it was earlier known as Connelly's Tavern.[41]

A Philadelphia lawyer gave his surname to Doran, situated in Tazewell County. And the story of the establishing of Burke's Garden, named after James Burke, is fairly well known. Historian Hanson's description is very terse:

> *Exploring party 1748. Burke, axman
> or chain-carrier, planted peelings of
> potatoes from breakfast; covered with
> brush. Next year, party returned; found
> bed of potatoes growing; named Burke's
> Garden. Burke's Fort there in 1774.
> Broad oval valley, surrounding ridges
> about 1000 feet higher than floor of
> area.*[42]

Roark's Gap in Tazewell was mentioned as early as 1774. A family was killed in the 1780s by Shawnee warriors at Dry Fork of the Sandy River; they were the wife and children of James Roark.

Wise County, in far southwestern Virginia, was established relatively late, in 1856. In the 1830s, a Matthios Kelly had moved from Kentucky to near the Big Stone Gap where he owned a store. Kelly was born about 1797.

> *Callahan Creek is also in Wise, a few
> miles from the Kentucky border. Kelly's
> son, John, born in 1821, lived on
> Callahan Creek, and the Kelly branch of
> it is named for John. He and his large
> family operated a grist mill, as well as a
> forge and gunsmith shop, making "flint-
> lock rifles, bear traps and tools for the
> pioneer settlers."*[43]

There is a section of Rockingham County known as the Mountain Valley area, near the foothills of the western slope of the Massanutten range. It stretches from Athlone community to Fridley's

Gap. A commentator tells us:

> *Tradition is that when the Speck family moved to the area in the 1870s they named their home Athlone after Athlone, Ireland. Later when a post office was established here it was called Athlone.*[44]

> *(We should note also an Athlone Farm over in Amherst County. The older portion of the Federal-style farmhouse itself was built before 1815.)*[45]

This Mountain Valley area included a few O'Roarks. James O'Roark was a coffin-builder. Michael "Rorok" was one of the census takers in 1784. There was a Phillimon Rorok, as well. In other records we learn of an Eleanor in 1746, a Philip in 1766, and one Timothy in 1768. "There is a tradition that the first O'Roarks in this area were two brothers who came from Ireland."[46]

In the year 1791 William Leitch was born at Douglas Bridge, in County Tyrone. His birthplace was only some fifteen miles from Derry town, from which he sailed about 1812, arriving in Portland, Maine. He eventually made his way to Buckingham County in Virginia. Here he became a successful merchant, operating a general store. At his death in 1871 he was buried at Mt. Ida. He was a cousin to the "Orangedale Leitches" who became prominent citizens in Charlottesville. (See the Charlottesville-Albemarle County chapter.)

The tiny Greene County community of McMullen derived its name from a Dublin immigrant,

John McMullan, who arrived in the American U.S. in 1760, making his way to Virginia. He became a soldier in the Revolutionary War; afterwards he moved to Georgia. His daughter and his son James remained in Greene County. Noted in the 1850 county census were four groups of McMullans, all listed as farmers/laborers.

The same census included some ten Sullivans, the oldest of them being a 45-year-old farmer, St. Clair Sullivan, who was born about 1805.

In a remote area of Greene County is a Sullivan graveyard, perched high on a hilltop on route 628; nearby are tiny Doylesville, the Lynch River, and Doyle's River. Some forty of the clan are interred here, all born in the 1800s. The first adult buried was Lydia Sullivan, who died in 1882. A prominent headstone reads:

T.H. SULLIVAN
1866-1892
KILLED ON R. R.

(The curious reader might examine Paudy Scully's book, *I Forgive Them All—The Judgement of John Twiss*. Scully imagines a central character, John Sullivan, as born in 1853 in tiny Ivy, Virginia, only a few miles from this Sullivan cemetery.

He traveled with false papers and he landed in Ireland where the Land War was at its height. He threw himself body and soul into the fight, first mainly on the political side.)[47]

In 1785 a Samuel Keane emigrated with his family to settle in Alleghany County and was included in the 1840 local census. This county includes the community of Callaghan, where Denis Callaghan purchased some seventy acres in 1773. He married Margaret Atkinson in 1786, and he lived until 1846/7. A son John became the operator of O'Callaghan's Tavern on the death of his father. John apparently was the county sheriff and Justice of the Peace; born in 1787, he married Maria Pulliam in Fredericksburg, and he died in 1862. Another son Charles lived from 1789 until 1864. Oliver Callaghan, probably another son, was the Clerk of the Circuit Court; his dates are 1798 to 1872.

At the point where Virginia, North Carolina, and Tennessee meet, lies McQueen Gap, which is in Washington County. In 1783, a sixty-acre parcel in the county was surveyed for a Patrick Denny on behalf of a John Donnell. This land was near the Clinch River. Toole Creek and Casey Hollow are also in this Virginia county, and a new Carrickfergus was intended to be situated there, too, with a link to the ancient town by that name in northeastern Ireland.

In 1794, four Irish immigrants in the county court swore their allegiance to the Commonwealth of Virginia: William King, James Caldwell, Samuel Bredin, and James Bredin. King was one of a group of thirty-nine people who in 1801 attempted to found a new town in the county, to be called Carrickfergus. Some forty-one lots were measured off in a location along the Holston River. Each lot of one-half acre was to have a frame, stone, or brick house erected. This early planned community failed to materialize, although a state map of about 1807 did carry that name, Carrickfergus, according to Mary Kegley, noted researcher, attorney, and archivist.[48]

Martin Burns, an immigrant from Sligo, died at 1853 at the age of sixty-four. His obituary in a Richmond newspaper included the following details:

> *Having received a liberal education in his native country, he emigrated to British America in the summer of 1818, where he remained a short time, removing to Virginia in 1819, since which time he has been employed as a teacher in Cumberland County, with the exception of one year in Bedford.*[49]

Numerous Moravians traveled through the region now known as Rockingham County in the mid-eighteenth century. According to an entry in a diary kept by one of these "zealous heralds of the cross,"

> *At night about* [April 1, 1748] *I lodged in a very disorderly, wicked and godless house of an Irishman, who kept an inn. The Saviour helped me through.*[50]

This rowdy wayside inn was located near Timberville.

In the eighteenth century Irish wayfarers were settling in Fauquier County, as noted in local legal documents. A landowner, one James Foley, was there by 1770; he married Elizabeth Ogelby in 1786, and a John Foley had married one Milly Ashby in 1766. Nuptials were also performed for Patrick Whalon, Bathsheba Hogan, Betty O'Banon, Benjamin Mahoney, Thomas Dennahy, Lettice Riley, and their respective wives and husbands.

Another land-grantee in the 1760s was William O'Bannon; the O'Bannons made their mark early in Fauquier:

> The first to apply for a grant in the Broad Run Valley with the avowed intention of living on his land was Bryan O'Bannon. His grant [was] dated 26 June 1728.
> ...Bryan O'Bannon was an Irishman, who, according to family tradition, came to Virginia about 1702.

(He was probably born in 1683.) His patent "almost totally encompasses the area known as the Great Meadow today." His will was dated 1760, and his six children inherited his estate, his wife having pre-deceased him.[51]

Irish Creek begins its flow in the Blue Ridge Mountains and within a few miles joins the South River. Irish Creek Valley, only some fifteen miles in length, lies in eastern Rockbridge County.

A family called Clark appeared in the Irish Creek section about 1810: "Family tradition records that the Clarks came from Ireland and lived for a short time in Henrico County. They settled in Pedlar in Amherst County."[52]

An early owner of Athlone farm was Thomas Clark, according to the 1759 Amherst County deed book. Among these numerous Irish Creek Clarks

was one Joseph Clark (1825-1886), who inherited more than one hundred acres from his father.
Joseph also may be the central figure of a well-
known ballad, according to a family archivist:

> *The Clark family has been forever
> immortalized in the song "Old Joe Clark"
> written by a sawmill hand, Samuel
> Downey. [Sam] could neither read nor
> write and drove a horse team up and
> down the mountains of Irish Creek Valley
> dragging logs to the mills. A natural
> banjo player, he often composed songs
> while driving his horses.*[53]

There are pertinent, Irish-flavored marriage
license bonds from Amherst County of the eighteenth century. Among them:

> *Elizabeth Moran and John Bolling in 1793*
> *Edmund Coffey and Tilda Fitzgerald in 1798*
> *James Gahagen and Elizabeth Murrell in 1798*
> *Benjamin Kelley and Nancy Jarrell in 1790*
> *John Lonogan and Elizabeth Stratton in 1789*
> *John Phelan and Salley Haines in 1793*
> *Jane Fitzpatrick and Charles Bailey in 1800*

Various Fitzpatricks and Fitzgeralds settled
in the eighteenth and nineteenth centuries in
Amherst, Nelson, Augusta, and Albemarle counties.

The immense geographical stretch of the original Augusta County was settled by large numbers
of English, German, Irish, and ScotsIrish, as they
came to call themselves from the mid-1800s. See

Lyman Chalkley's three-volume compilation, *The Chronicles of the Scotch-Irish Settlement in Virginia.*[54]

The huge Beverley Patent of the 1730s included some 2,000 acres which were deeded to John Lewis, and "the land which eventually became downtown Waynesboro was deeded to one Daniel Monohan" in that same decade.[55]

Augusta and Albemarle counties meet at the summit of Afton Mountain in the Blue Ridge chain. In the 1850s, a series of four railway tunnels was dug through Afton; the longest tunnel stretched some four thousand feet. The bulk of the incredibly tedious labor was done by Irish workers, who used picks, hand drills, and black powder to bore through solid rock. This phenomenal engineering feat saw the deaths of many men; they will be cited in the tunnels section of the Albemarle chapter, along with those who died from cholera during the project.

The number of Irish people in nineteenth-century Wythe County presents a conundrum of sorts. The cemetery of St. Patrick's Church in the Speedwell community contains the remains of more than forty of Irish extraction, and St. Mary's Church graveyard in Wytheville is the resting-place of more than seventy Irish.

Prominent local historian Mary Kegley has scoured church, court, and cemetery records in the county. She has documented some 140 Irish immigrants who came from thirteen counties, Rathlin Island, and the cities of Belfast and Dublin. Her conclusion:

> The biggest puzzle at the moment is
> why so many chose our county. Often
> it has been said that they came to work
> on the railroad or at the mines, but
> census occupations do not confirm this.
> Furthermore, many others suggested the
> Irish came as a result of the famine, but
> many were here before that event.[56]

Only a few county arrivals can be traced to the eighteenth century. Margaret Carroll was born in 1795, John Carroll in 1799. Both these natives of County Tyrone are interred at St. Mary's.

Alexander Smith arrived in 1792 in Wytheville, where he began his law practice. He was a native of Rathlin Island (off the upper coast of County Antrim), where he was born in 1765. He served in the Virginia legislature for several terms, rose to the rank of Brigadier General during the War of 1812, and then served in the U.S. Congress. He was buried in Washington on his death in 1830.[57]

We could speak of a Wythe "Irish triangle." Speedwell is situated only about fifteen miles south of Wytheville on highway 21, and Murpheyville is located some fifteen miles west of Wytheville.

In 1842, Bishop Whelan of Richmond visited Wytheville, where he received some converts into the Catholic church and authorized a mission. Among the new members was Sheriff Matthews, who made a financial donation and set aside an acre of ground for a chapel. The bishop returned the following year and "delivered a course of lectures which were well received by the townspeople." In 1845, the bishop was able to dedicate St. Mary's in Wytheville.[58] Some thirty years later the second Catholic church, St. Patrick's, was organized in Speedwell.

In the graveyard attached to St. Joseph's Church in the town of Petersburg, there are two dozen or more nineteenth-century headstones, suggesting an Irish presence related probably to the huge Famine of the 1840s in Ireland. The burials were for a Bannon, native of Dublin; a Dorsy from Wicklow, a Finn from Kilkenny, a Hanrahan from Limerick, a Kearney from Tipperary, a McFail from Longford, a Sexton from Cork, and a Walsh from Kerry. Other headstones are inscribed Burk, Curtin, Dolan, Ferrell, Halligan, Kenney, McManamin, Moran, O'Brien, Rahily, Sheehy, and Sheinnov.

All in all, virtually every county in Virginia has seen an Irish presence in the past four centuries. Michael J. O'Brien's research efforts for seventeenth and eighteenth century land-grants covered some thirty-three counties. William J. Sweeny's research pertains to the same era, and the volumes of the *Journal of the American – Irish Historical Society* contain material from both of these researchers.

Endnotes

1. *Journal of the Historical Society of Fairfax County Virginia*, Vol.17 (1981), pp. 39–64.
2. *Journal... Fairfax County*, pp. 65–73.
3. Wesley E. Pippenger, *Marriage and Death Notices from Alexandria, VA, Newspapers, Vol.I, 1784–1838* (Arlington, Va.: Pippenger, 2005), p. 3.
4. Pippenger, *Marriage and Death Notices*, p. 64.
5. Pippenger, *Marriage and Death Notices*, p. 95.
6. Pippenger, *Marriage and Death Notices*, p. 117.
7. Pippenger, *Marriage and Death Notices*, p. 143.
8. Pippenger, *Marriage and Death Notices*, p. 150.
9. Pippenger, *Marriage and Death Notices*, p. 167.
10. Pippenger, *Marriage and Death Notices*, p. 230.
11. Pippenger, *Marriage and Death Notices*, p. 271.
12. Letter of October 7, 1997, to Kevin Donleavy.
13. *The Alexandria Times and District of Columbia Daily Advertiser*, Thursday, December 5, 1799.
14. Arthur Leslie Keith, "The McCarthy Family," *William and Mary Quarterly, II,* Vol. 2, (1922), pp. 119-132.
15. *Calendar of State Papers*, Vol. 6 , pp. 701–2.
16. David Longshore, *Encyclopedia of Hurricanes, Typhoons, and Cyclones* (New York: Facts on File, 1998), p. 329.
17. Issue of February 11, 1773, cited in Donald G. Shomette, *Shipwrecks on the Potomac* (Centreville, MD.: Tidewater Publishers, 1982), pp. 20–21.
18. Westmoreland County, Virginia 1665–1677 *Deeds, Patents, Wills*, cited at Google, Irish Westmoreland Va.
19. John Bennett Boddie, *Southside Virginia Families*, Vol.1 (Baltimore, MD: Genealogical Publishing Company, 1955), p. 380.
20. Ronald L. Hurst, "Irish Influences on Cabinetmaking in Virginia's Rappahannock River Basin," in *American Furniture* 1997.
21. *1783 Taxlist of Upper District of Lunenberg Parish.*
22. Michael J. O'Brien, *Journal of the American Irish Historical Society*, various volumes.
23. Jerrilyn Eby, *They Called Stafford Home* (Bowie, MD.: Heritage Publishing, 1997), pp. 181–2.
24. Eby, *They Called Stafford Home*, pp. 354–6.
25. Eby, *They Called Stafford Home*, p. 80.
26. Eby, *They Called Stafford Home*, p. 99.
27. James Hagemann, *The Heritage of Virginia* (Norfolk, VA: Donning,

1986), p.73.

28. Rosewell Page, *Hanover County — Its History and Legends* (private printing, 1926), p. 26.

29. Hagemann, p.156, points to Tobias McGahey. But his name is given as William McGahey in Hanson, cited herein.

30. Ann L. Miller, *Antebellum Orange* (Orange, VA: Historical Society, 1988), p. 56.

31. Raus McDill Hanson, *Virginia Place Names* (Verona, VA.: McClure Press, 1969), p. 52.

32. Hanson, *Virginia Place Names*, p. 152.

33. Hanson, *Virginia Place Names*, p. 155.

34. Hanson, *Virginia Place Names*, p. 169.

35. H. Jackson Darst, *Dublin and the Darsts* (Newbern, VA.: Wilderness Road Regional Museum, 1992), pp. 4, 13.

36. Hanson, *Virginia Place Names*, pp. 26, 51.

37. Hanson, *Virginia Place Names*, p. 5.

38. Virginia Davis, "35,000 Acres Were Bought On a $25 Bid," *Kingsport News*, Sunday, November 9, 1952.

39. Virginia Davis, "35,000 Acres Were Bought On a $25 Bid," *Kingsport News*, Sunday, November 9, 1952.

40. R.B. McDowell, "The Protestant Nation (1775–1800)," in *The Course of Irish History*, ed. T.W. Moody and F.X. Martin, eds. (Boulder, CO.: Roberts Rinehart, 1996), pp. 232–47. (Original edition, 1967).

41. Hanson, *Virginia Place Names*, p. 54.

42. Hanson, *Virginia Place Names*, pp. 203–4.

43. *Historical and Biographical Sketches* (Historical Society of Southwest Virginia), No. 6, March 1972, p. 37.

44. Mary Marie Koontz Arrington, *Mountain Valley People* (Baltimore, MD: Gateway Publications, 1982), p. 1.

45. Emmie Ferguson Farrar and Emilee Hines, *Old Virginia Houses— The Piedmont* (Verona, VA.: McClure Press,1969), p. 52.

46. Arrington, *Mountain Valley People*, p. 145.

47. Paudy Scully, *I Forgive Them All—The Judgement of John Twiss* (Herxheim, Germany: private printing, 2007), p. 14.

48. Mary B. Kegley, "Virginia and the Carrickfergus Connection," *Carrickfergus and District Historical Journal*, Vol. 8 (1995), pp. 22–3. Of these thirty-nine petitioners, William King and Connally Findley (both born in Ireland) became U.S. citizens.

49. Wesley E. Pippenger, *Death Notices from Richmond, Virginia Newspapers 1841–1853* (Richmond, VA: Virginia Genealogical Society, 2002).

50. John W. Wayland, *A History of Rockingham County* (Dayton, VA.:

Ruebush-Elkins Publishing, 1912), p.45.

51. Trudy J. Sundberg and John K. Gott, *Valiant Virginian—Story of Presley Neville O'Bannon* (Heritage Books, no place, no date).

52. Donna Huffer, *Fare Thee Well, Old Joe Clark: History of the Clark Family of Rockbridge County* (Churchville, VA.: private printing, 1991), pp. 4, 43.

53. Huffer, *Fare Thee Well*, p.43. Some old-time music scholars link this song to incidents in Pittsylvania County of the 1870s.

54. Lyman Chalkley, *Chronicles of the Scotch-Irish Settlement in Virginia: Extracted from the Original Court Documents of Augusta County 1745-1800*. Baltimore, MD.: Genealogy Publishing Co., 1989. 3 volumes.

55. George R. Hawke, *A History of Waynesboro, Virginia to 1900* (Waynesboro, VA: Historical Commission, 1997), pp.8–9.

56. Letter of April 20, 2006 from Mary Kegley to Kevin Donleavy.

57. *Wythe County Historical Review*, Vol.24, July 1983.

58. James H. Bailey, *A History of the Diocese of Richmond—The Formative Years* (Richmond, VA: Diocese of Richmond, 1956), p.92.

CHAPTER 6

Charlottesville Town, Albemarle County, and Thomas Jefferson

The eighteenth century saw the first influx of Irish people into the Albemarle County area. Charles Lynch took out a land patent in 1733 for some 800 acres in what is now the Pen Park section. Patrick Nowland obtained some 400 acres in 1737, and Hugh Dohorty was granted land rights that same year for his 600 acres.

The next decade, several Fitzgeralds obtained more than 2,800 acres, James Ireland came into 450 acres in 1748, Joseph Fitzpatrick in 1746 claimed 800 acres, and a kinsman, Thomas Fitzpatrick, was granted his own 800 acres the same year. Dennis Doyle patented some 800 acres in 1741 in northwestern Albemarle, and his land included what has been known to the present-day as Doyle's River.

The landowner James Ireland is noted thusly in Edgar Woods's study: "The road which passes over the Green Mountain...was established at an early date. For many years it was known as the Irish Road,...for a man named James Ireland, who was a patentee in that neighborhood."[1] Irish Road stretches west from the town of Scottsville, and has retained its name for some two hundred and fifty years.

One of the few comments which pertain to any eighteenth-century Albemarle Irishry comes from the Reverend Edgar Woods, who informs us that one Dennis Doyle "appears to have been a man of means, and to have been still living in the country in 1760; as in that year was born within its limits John Doyle, who was in all probability a son of Dennis." This Doyle removed to Kentucky, was a county magistrate there for some twenty years, and died there in 1847.[2]

Other land grants went to Luke Carroll (400 acres in 1750), Edward Cartee or McCarty (60 acres in 1758), John Moran (280 acres in 1759) and John P. Burke (440 acres 1760).

The Fitzpatricks were somewhat numerous in the area. Thomas Jefferson in his Memorandum Book of 1769 mentions John and Joseph having over 200 acres on the Hardware River near Thomas Fitzpatrick's land. In 1782, John was certified on the tax list as owning six slaves and twenty cows. Thomas married a Frances Gentry in 1787, and two years later John married Jean Blaine. This large clan also included Edward, Hamner, and William Fitzpatrick. Ruth Fitzpatrick was wed to a William Moran in 1805.

Charles Lynch eventually came to own some 6,500 acres in the town and county "and on the waters of Mechum's not far from the Blue Ridge [Mountains]."[3] Charles served as a county magistrate in the mid-1700s, and moved eventually to what came to be called Lynchburg (see the chapter by that name), where he would come to own some

1,600 acres at his death in 1753.

Charles was born about 1705 in Galway. He had emigrated from Ireland about 1720 as a servant indentured to a Quaker family, the Clarks, and he represented Albemarle County 1748-49 in the state House of Burgesses. He married Sarah Clark, whose father Christopher in 1742 bought land east of Charlottesville (now the Ben Coolyn, Bridle Spur, and Tall Oaks estates). The Clarks and the Lynches became slave owners and some of Charles' slaves worked at the ferry he owned on the local Rivanna River.

Local Albemarle marriages reveal more eighteenth-century names:

Ann Grady married (1791) Peter Reily.
James Farrel married (1786) Mary Wells.
Nancy Nolan married (1797) Younger Grady.
Lawrence Fitzgarald married (1796) Suzannah Hill.
Daniel Donovan married (1792) Nancy Rae.
John Toole married (1788) Sarah Moran.
Patrick Ryan married (1788) Nancy Thomason.

Other residents called Grady lived in the area, probably close kin to Ann and Younger. There was Jesse Grady, who married Polly Hoy in 1807, as well as Reuben Grady, who wed Nancy Reid in 1808. At Oakwood Cemetery in Charlottesville are interred eight Gradys, including Daniel, Willie, and William, born in the mid-1800s.

Edmond Grady in 1787 served as a witness to

the marriage of Sally Grady, described as a "spinster".

Thomas Grady, who apparently died in 1841, was among the ninety or more signers of the "Save Mr. Jefferson's Bust! An Albemarle Petition of 1827." (Other pertinent signers were Joseph Antrim, "Hew Chilosm", Mathew Casey, Edward Coles, James Dinsmore, William Flanaghan, John Leitch, and George Toole. All will be cited in this chapter.) There was one Joshua Grady who died in 1794; he had a daughter Mary. Apparently there was another Joshua Grady who had a blacksmith shop in the 1830s. Local historian James Alexander wrote of an early Charlottesville landmark on Market St.:

> *The old Stone Tavern, or as it was*
> *called, the Central Hotel, built in 1806*
> *by the late James Monroe. ...the late Mr.*
> *Thomas Grady was...bar-keeper and*
> *chief manager.*[4]

Another probable kinsman was a Joseph Grady, who in 1798 purchased 100 acres on Contrary Creek in adjacent Louisa County from a William Hughes for the price of sixteen pounds.

Quite a few Sullivans arrived early in the area, although virtually none are buried in Charlottesville. Between 1793 and 1830 Albemarle archives recorded the marriages of the following Sullivans: Daniel, David, Dennis, Elizabeth, Jeremiah, Mary Ann, Polly, Sinclair, Thomas, and William. The federal census of 1810 recorded that Albemarle residents Derby Sullivan owned no slaves, nor did

Richard Sullivan. Derby, also known as Darby the Younger, was apparently born prior to 1765, and came to Albemarle by 1791. His uncle, also Darby, lived in Stafford County.

(Other Sullivans became landowners in the 1600s and 1700s in Westmoreland, Rappahannock, Northumberland, Essex, and Lancaster Counties.)

Stephen R. Sullivan was a Charlottesville carriage-maker in the early 1800s. His business seems to have been located on the north side of what is now West Main Street, in the larger Vinegar Hill area.

Then there is the miniscule area of Greene County, mere yards from the northwestern Albemarle border, a place known as Sullivans. In the nineteenth century, the Sullivan general store (still standing) also served as the Sullivans post office. There now is a well-maintained boneyard, surrounded by a chain-link fence. The cemetery contains graves of some forty people, nearly all of them Sullivans of the nineteenth century. Nearby are Doyle's River, Lynch's River, and Doylestown.

James Flannagan, born in Dublin in 1730, was brought as an infant by his father Ambrose and his mother (unnamed) to Virginia; by the 1740s the family (originally from County Roscommon) had settled in Fluvanna County. Louisa County records indicate that some 400 acres went to a James Flanagan in 1747, land in the vicinity of local routes 22 and 15.

Another archive shows that one James Flannagan (born in Albemarle County in 1754) married

Polly (or Phoebe) Simpson; his father was listed as the Dublin-born James senior. And a James Flannagan was wed to a Mary Bowles Johnson.

In 1841, Benjamin Collins Flannagan took a wife, as did William Flannagan in 1846. Their ancestor was the 1730 emigrant, James Flannagan. In 1850 Benjamin and his wife lived at "Bona Hora", a fine house with classical features on Lyons Court; he owned some twenty-one acres in this section of Charlottesville. Benjamin "was a cashier in the Monticello Bank and owned a brick factory at Buck Island."[5]

During the construction of the Bremo mansion on the James River in the early 1800s, a master plasterer there was a Flanagan, probably a kinsman of these other Flannagans. (More Irish elements in the building of Bremo are covered later in this chapter.)

The Maplewood Cemetery is the final resting place of some fifteen Flanagans/Flannagans, while at Oakwood Cemetery there are ten or more Flannagans, including one James, who lived from 1822 to 1905.

Among the dozen or so early Irish workers at the University of Virginia, we find that an Ambrose Flanagan provided "lumber, [and] Roman cement".[6]

Finally, there is a small creek to the northeast of Charlottesville named Flannigan Branch.

One of the members of the United Irishman group in Dublin in the 1790s was one David Fitzgerald. In nearby County Wexford, one of the UI militants there was Edward Fitzgerald, of the landed gentry.

The Fitzgerald surname has been fairly common in Virginia in Albemarle, Nelson, Rockbridge, and Augusta counties since the eighteenth century. Albemarle was established as a county in 1744, and in 1761 two counties were formed from its lower portion, Amherst and Buckingham.

Among the early Albemarle settlers with the surname Fitzgerald were: Lawrence, who obtained some 610 acres; Joseph (born in 1730), who by 1747 had some 360 acres; James C. (born about 1788); Thomas, who by 1756 had some 1,660 acres; and William, who owned 400 acres in 1781.

Nelson was established as a county in 1808, formed from Amherst County. In Nelson, there are at least seven known Fitzgerald graveyards. About 1740 a James Fitzgerald received a Nelson land grant.

One chronicler of his family's history, Robert Fitzgerald, notes: "...my roots in Nelson County go [deep]...their predecessors came from Ireland, Scotland, England, and France."[7]

The Bedford County federal census of 1850 details several Fitzgeralds: John, 22, born in Ireland; Patrick, 24, born in Ireland; William, 27, born in Ireland. In Botetourt County, according to the 1850 census, there were Irish-born Fitzgeralds: Joseph, 25; another Joseph, 24; and a John, 30.

Noted in the 1860 Lexington town census was one Thomas Fitzgerald, born in Ireland, 47, a "day laborer." With his wife Ellen, 45, they had 3 teenage children. They lived near Mary, 65, as well as John, 30, (a gardener), and his wife Kate, 30, all born in Ireland.

In 1635, one Redmond Fitzgerald was brought as an indentured servant to Warrasquinoake County. There was a "Fitzjarrell" cited in the 1700s Bristol parish on the eastern coast of Virginia. One John Fitzgerald was granted 1,430 acres in the 1720s in Prince George County. Ann Fitzgerald was married in 1792 in Westmoreland County. And a John Fitzgerald was a land-holder in Essex County in the 1720s.[8]

There were some Fitzgeralds who came to Lynchburg. A headstone for Nancy "Fitzgerrald" was carved by a Fagan in 1853 (see Lynchburg chapter for more Fagans). David Fitzgerald applied for citizenship in 1851, as did William. William claimed to have been born in Cork in 1823, and David claimed an 1830 birth in Kerry. On the April 1851 canal payroll, for work near Lynchburg, a John Fitzgerald was included on the workers' payroll.

As a final note on the Irishness of the Fitzgeralds, one Dorsey Bell Fitzgerald (1872-1925) "was born on Irish Creek in Rockbridge County just below the Grant Family Cemetery where he is buried."[9]

The saga of the Butler family in Charlottesville can be only roughly sketched at this point in time.

According to family lore, cabinet-maker Edward Butler and his wife Charity emigrated from Ireland to Campbell County. In the 1770s, Edward bought the half-acre "lott. no. 4" in the center of tiny Charlottesville, and built their house about 1785 (it is now 410 East Jefferson Street). The house is of brick, a Georgian edifice of two stories.[10]

Edward's anti-monarchical views are apparent in two documents to which he is a signatory. In 1779, the "Oath of Allegiance Signed by Citizens of Albemarle County" included the signatures of Edward and others of an Irish orientation: Joseph Nielson, John Fitzpatrick, Benjamin Lacey, John Coles, Thomas West, Wittie (Wittle) Flannagan, James McMannus, Lit F Sullevan, Richard Watson, Matthew Maury, and Thomas Jefferson himself. In total, over two hundred locals put their names to this document.

In 1777 Edward Butler (along with other citizens) pledged 10 shillings to support a progressive clergyman. The group approved of the "political conduct" of the Reverend Mr. Charles Clay, in "rejecting the tyrant and tyranny of Britain."

Edward Butler gave the house and land on East Jefferson Street to a son, James, in 1791, the year the latter came to Charlottesville. James seems to have been a political refugee of the United Irishman movement. He lived "in hiding in Albemarle the remainder of his life," in the words of the family historian:

"It was a tradition in our family that James Butler fled Ireland with a price on his head, under an alias... He may have been involved in some business with Wolfe Tone."[11]

James used the surnames Nolly and Notley, and in 1807 married Susan Ropon, the same year that James and Edward witnessed the marriage of Peggy Butler, who was perhaps James' sister. The following year, local records note that James and Susan/Susanne sold the East Jefferson property to local man John Kelly for some $550.

The Butlers' link to Campbell County (near Lynchburg) is intriguing. In 1783, Edward is listed in the "Citizens of Campbell County" who had provided support against the English during the Revolution. A few decades later, an Edward and a James Butler are enumerated in the 1820 census of Carroll County. Yet in Charlottesville, David Fowler married James' widow Susan in 1814.

The two oldest Charlottesville cemeteries are full of Irish-born and Irish-Americans, some sixty or more individuals. There are headstones in Oakwood Cemetery for eight of the local Grady clan, including James J. Grady (1822-1905); ten Flannagans; John O'Toole, "Artist Born in Dublin, Ireland"; O'Donnell and Quinn individuals; a few members of the Leitch family; and John Gorman, stone-mason highly regarded by Thomas Jefferson. Rebecca Leitch ("consort of Samuel") was born in Ireland and is interred at Oakwood; her dates are 1783-1820.

Maplewood Cemetery is the resting-place for Samuel (1790-1870) and other Leitches from County Tyrone. They include Andrew, born in 1804 (his father died in 1823), and James, American-born in 1814. James' wife Anne (born an O'Toole) lies beside him: she was born in 1811. And Isabella (born in 1814) is also in this plot. Mary Leitch was born in 1816.

Other Maplewood headstones provide more

insight to these early Irish. Influential John Kelly is here: 1766-1830 (more of him later); and T.H. Hayes from County Tipperary, 1834-1888. There are the previously mentioned Flanagans/Flannagans, sixteen Antrims, and nineteen Watsons some of whom were from County Tyrone. There is also Jane Hagan. "a native of Ireland," 1783-1869. John O'Connor ("son of John and Anne Ledwedge O'Connor of Dublin, Ireland") is here; he was born in 1827. Cornelius Galvin from Cork died at age thirty-three. Other nineteenth-century individuals here are John L. O'Neale, Thomas McManus, and John McKenna and his wife Elizabeth Wood.

Regarding the several Watsons, historian Edgar Woods records a useful link for us:

Joseph Watson, an immigrant from Ireland, in 1832 bought from Andrew Leitch, agent of the Dinsmore estate, Orangedale, where he lived until his death several years ago. His wife was Ellen Leitch, a sister of Samuel Leitch Jr.[12]

Joseph was born circa 1790; Ellen lived from 1784 to 1849. Andrew, probably her brother, married Mary Watson (Joseph's sister born 1816) in 1848. Mary and Joseph were from County Tyrone; he lived 1784-1872.

Of the physician, Dr. James Leitch, we learn an anecdote revealed by another local commentator:

"Then a young practitioner, full of humor, he

kept chained up a tame bear that often got loose and troubled the neighbors."[13]

Two of the older Leitches, brothers James and Samuel (James married Polly Lewis in 1811), owned shops on the east side of Court Square in Charlottesville. Of this Samuel, commentator James Alexander tells us that "young Mr. Leitch was sociable, friendly, hospitable and enthusiastic in whatever he engaged in... He served a number of years as alderman in Charlottesville."[14]

Mathew Casey's signature on the 1827 petition to preserve the bust of Thomas Jefferson (who died 1826) suggests his civic presence. He had also published a notice in the *Central Gazette* that he "wishes to employ two or three Journeymen Boot and Shoemakers" for his Charlottesville shop (issue of July 12, 1822). Historian Alexander describes Mathew thusly: "an Irishman, whose family afterwards removed to St. Louis, Missouri." He adds that one of Casey's sons remained in town, and "carried on the cabinet making business, and was a skillful and neat workman."[15] There was also a Dennis Casey living in town, possibly a kinsman.

One of the Albemarle County marriages of 1820 was between an Elizabeth McDonnell (or McCarnelle) and a Daniel Keith. Alexander describes Keith as "an Irishman, who acted in the capacity of constable" in the community.[16] One ponders whether the constable was related to some rebel/Jacobite Keiths who emigrated or were deported from Scotland in the early eighteenth century.

At one point, Keith lived in the brick house (at

Market and East Third Streets) where Dr. Leitch and his bear later dwelt. In the 1830s, Keith was a printer in town. In 1841 he purchased what is now known as the Nimmo or Keith House on Keith Valley Road. His son James lived there at one point; his trade was that of stonemason. The house itself must date from the mid-1700s. Oddly enough, the 1850 census in nearby Augusta County reveals a Daniel Keith (age thirty) who listed his trade as a laborer.

In the old section of Charlottesville, the courthouse square was the center of town. Adjacent to the square was McKee's Row, a single block that melded homes and shops. (See the 1818 map of the town). Andrew McKee lived here; he's buried at Maplewood (1780-1849) alongside Martha Gannon McKee (1774-1829). Others on that block were the elder James Leitch, who lived there in the 1820s, John Kelly, Mathew Casey, and George O'Toole.

From McKee's Row could be seen the Butlers' house, the courthouse itself, and within a few hundred yards the shops run by the Leitches. The reader is directed to "A View of Charlottesville, Va circa 1828" available for copying at the local historical society. This bird's-eye item includes some fifty-eight houses and shops as noted by historian James Alexander. Among these venues are eleven with an Irish connection; it is well to keep in mind that the town's population had only slowly increased from about two hundred in 1790 to only some three hundred in the 1820s.

A minor but energetic figure—that seems to be

one Patrick Quinn. At one point he is noticed as a toll-gate man by commentator Edgar Woods:

"The first gate west of town was immediately opposite the large oak tree on Jesse Lewis' place..., and which was blown down by a violent storm in September 1896; its keeper was Patrick Quinn."[17]

There was an M. Quinn who worked as a brick-maker in 1824 during the construction of the new University of Virginia. Perhaps he is the father of a man buried at Riverview Cemetery: Michael Quinn (1852-1912), who married Mary Ann O'Donnell (1861-1957). Perhaps a different Patrick Quinn was listed in the 1860 census of nearby Rockbridge County as a "day laborer," age 45. He and his wife Jane in 1854 lost an infant daughter to dysentery.

In 1843 in Lynchburg, a Repeal Association was formed, and a Patrick Quinn was the secretary. (See the Lynchburg chapter). The organization raised support to condemn and repeal the union of Ireland with England, which came into law in 1801. In 1841 Patrick married Constance, daughter of Mary Dornin; Mary was very active on the Irish cultural front in Lynchburg. In 1842, this Patrick Quinn applied for U.S. citizenship: files number 1029 and number 1051.

The earliest mention of the O'Toole family is in the 1790 Albemarle census, which cites a John Toole as head of a household. A probable kinsman was another John Toole, who held the rank of Major in the Dublin unit of the forces of the United Irish-men in the same decade.

One Michael O'Toole was a professor of chemistry who perished in a laboratory explosion when he was teaching in Dublin. His widow came to live in Charlottesville in 1827 with their three children. One daughter Anne married James A. Leitch in 1835, one of the County Tyrone Leitches living in Charlottesville. One son Jeremiah worked in his uncle George Toole's grocery shop, probably located on West Main Street. George was a brother of Michael and lived 1778-1856.

This Jeremiah Toole used to regale town residents "about the Irish patriots, Thomas Addis Emmet and Daniel O'Connell." [18] Jerry eventually took up a printer's job in Petersburg.

Michael O'Toole's other son was John (1815-1860), who achieved considerable fame as a portraitist in Virginia. There are some three hundred of his paintings hanging throughout the state. The curious reader is directed to his biography: William B. O'Neal, *Primitive Into Painter: Life and Letters of John Toole* (University of

John Toole, Daguerreotype

Virginia Press, 1960). A hint of political leanings in the O'Toole clann rests in the fact that John drew a portrait of John Philpot Curran (now archived in the University art museum). It is based on the likeness of Curran in R.R. Madden's celebrated study of the United Irishmen. Curran was the most prominent legal defender of the UI who were tried in Dublin courts.

John Toole also painted James Alexander, the local historian who noted that the old Vinegar Hill section of Charlottesville was given its name by George O'Toole, "and he named it in honor of the Vinegar Hill in Ireland, where the O'Tooles lived." This historian also wrote of Charlottesville "There was a saying that the O'Tooles, the O'Traceys and the O'Donovans ruled Vinegar Hill."[19] George O'Toole also operated a tailor's shop. In 1824, he had for rent "2 brick Houses at the west end of Charlottesville." [20]

This Charlottesville set of Tooles/O'Tooles came from County Wicklow. In his will of 1856, George leaves bequests to "Pat Toole Aughran [sic] County Wicklow Ireland", and to Terry Toole, also of Aughrim.

This small town lies in south Wicklow, near the border with County Wexford, and a present-day town establishment is named "O'Toole's Traditional Pub." Two bridges over the Aughrim River which flows through the town have historical markers referring to the 1798 Rising. One plaque honors local heroic fighter Anne Devlin. The other commemorates the Battle of Aughrim, when General Joseph Holt's United Irishmen fought the English troops. Aughrim town is some fifty miles south of

Dublin, and a mere thirty-five miles from Enniscorthy in County Wexford. All local families would know of such 1798 battles in Tullow, Vinegar Hill, New Ross, etc., against the English.

One chronicler of 1798 cites "heroines like...Susy Toole, the Wicklow blacksmith's daughter."[21]

There was another noted O'Toole, "a small farmer living in Castlemore Cross Roads" in adjoining County Carlow.[22] He protected two UI members, who were ultimately found and hanged: Father John Murphy and one Gallagher.

Annalists, chroniclers, and historians agree that when the O'Tooles were driven by the Anglo-Normans out of County Kildare into Wicklow, they never forgot their ancestral homelands. The 1200s and 1300s, especially, are replete with incidents against the Crown. The O'Tooles in Charlottesville doubtless knew of "Black Monday" in 1209, when the dispossessed clanns of O'Tooles and O'Byrnes killed some three hundred English at Cullenswood (Fiodh Chuilinn) near Dublin, even today referred to as the Bloody Fields.

In 1835, a Charlottesville pair were married. Anne Toole became the partner of James Leitch. It was a quiet, but symbolic, event. In this new world, there was no insurmountable difficulty in a Wicklow Catholic woman marrying a Tyrone Protestant man. Much historical baggage was left behind. An O'Toole wasn't harassed by the English, nor was a Leitch driven to uphold the English Crown.

Most of the Charlottesville Irish just cited lived and worked as townspeople of modest means. They might own small shops and be proud of their small houses. Their social circles were modest, as well.

The Coles arrived with gold in store. Major elements of this Anglo-Irish family's history stand in clear contrast to that of the Caseys, Butlers, Watsons, and O'Tooles.

John Coles (circa 1705-1747) emigrated in the 1730s and settled in Richmond, where, within a very few years, he purchased some fifteen newly laid-out building lots. He soon was able to set up what he called a summer home, Enniscorthy, on three thousand acres in the Green Mountain section of Albemarle, a few miles south of Charlottesville. Of this Green Mountain land, he ultimately assigned estates and "big houses" to his offspring.

John's father Walter Coles was born near Enniscorthy in County Wexford, although the family came to land in Ireland in the mid-1600s:

> *The Coles Family of Virginia is of English descent. At an early date, when the English Government, in order to subjugate Ireland and to render it, if possible, obedient to the laws of England, offered large inducements to English gentlemen to emigrate, one of the ancestors of the present Virginia branch removed to Enniscorthy.*[23]

Walter Coles was for several decades a preeminent figure in Enniscorthy town, being Provost (chief Customs official) of the town. At some point, others in the Coles clann lived in the nearby town of Gorey. The family historian in Virginia surmises

that there were some Coles individuals killed when
the Irish rose in 1798 in County Wexford: the early
Coles certainly would have known of the two thousand Irish killed in County Wexford by the English during the insurrection of the 1640s. There was
a small village called Colestown close to Wexford
town.

The second John Coles became very prominent
in Albemarle County affairs, and was on good social
terms with Thomas Jefferson. He inherited Enniscorthy House and land from his father. By the 1780s,
this John II owned seventy-one slaves. The house
was completely destroyed by fire in 1839, and the
present splendid brick edifice was built in 1850.[24]

By contrast, let us consider, Dear Reader, a son of
John II, one Edward, born at Enniscorthy estate. In
1819, Edward raised every white eyebrow in Albemarle County when he moved with all his inherited
slaves out to Illinois. There he freed them, and gave
each slave family one hundred and sixty acres of
land. Running on an anti-slavery platform, Edward
Coles was elected governor of Illinois in 1822.[25]

There were seven noted Irish artisans who
worked on Thomas Jefferson's major architectural
projects: Monticello, his home; the University of
Virginia; and Poplar Forest, his stately retreat.
(The last is located ninety miles south of Monticello
in Bedford County.)

John Gorman, born in Ireland about 1786, emigrated to Lynchburg. He was an excellent stone-
cutter who worked at Poplar Forest before he came
to do stone work at the University in 1819. He died

in 1827 at age forty-one and is interred at Riverview Cemetery in Charlottesville. He left a widow,
Roseanna, and a child, Mary Ann.

Joseph Antrim, born in the 1780s, was a master
plasterer at Poplar Forest and at the University.
Described as "an Irishman who owned 246 acres
in the county" [26] of Albemarle (which he bought in
1822), he died in 1843. He and his wife Susan probably lived north of Doylesville, their house being
called Walnut Level. There were several local kin:
in 1840 one John T. Antrim witnessed the marriage
of Hannah Antrim to a Levi Monroe. This John died
in 1884. There was a large general store in Charlottesville which was operated up into the 1880s by
one E.M. Antrim.

John Jordan was a skilled brick mason who
worked on both Monticello and the courthouse
in Charlottesville. "Of Irish descent, he was born
in 1777 in Goochland County and died in 1854,"
according to professor Edward Lay's description in
his study of local architecture.[27]

Lay in his book includes a portrait of Jordan,
and also one of Dabney Cosby. Cosby's masonry is
in evidence at the University. He was born in Louisa County in 1779, and died in Raleigh in 1862.
In Lay's description, "The Irish Cosbys had been in
Virginia since 1626."[28]

The Chisholm family lived east of Charlottesville, having originally emigrated from Scotland, to
northeastern Ireland, to Virginia. Lay's citation of
Hugh is complete: "Irishman Hugh Chisholm, born
in the 1770s, began working at Monticello in 1796,

occasionally with his brother, and also was employed as a brickmason, carpenter, and plasterer at Poplar Forest and Montpelier."[29] At the University, he did carpentry work. He executed the plaster work on Green Mountain (near Keene, south of Charlottesville) at a big house called Old Woodville, owned by one of the wealthy Coles clan.

A native of Ballymoney, County Antrim, James Dinsmore was naturalized in 1798 in Philadelphia. Thomas Jefferson met him there, and engaged him as a builder/master joiner at Monticello and the University. Dinsmore's efforts are best seen at Pavilions III, V, and VIII. He built a modest brick house for himself on some five hundred acres, calling it Orange Dale. He drowned in a local river in 1830.

Several examples of Dinsmore's work as designer/ builder have survived: two-story Oak Lawn near his own Orange Dale house, 1111 West Main (the Vowles townhouse), and the nearby Livers townhouse at 1211 West Main. Edward Lay describes as one of Dinsmore's "crowning achievements" the Estouteville estate (1827) on Green Mountain.[30] (There are photographs of these dwellings in Lay's book.)

The Dinsmore heirs sold part of Orange Dale to Joseph and Ellen Watson who lived there for many years. Joseph lived from 1784 to 1872; Ellen (nee Leitch) from 1784 to 1849. They had emigrated from County Tyrone.

Dinsmore's brother, a carpenter, killed himself after James' death. A third brother was William (circa 1780 to c. 1836), who played fiddle. He lived at Rock Hill estate, afterwards living at Orange Dale until his death.[31]

Dinsmore worked side by side with another County Antrim emigrant, John Nielson, at Monticello, the University, Montpelier, as well as Bremo estate, where Neilson's architectural vision is best seen. Both had architectural training, Neilson having been apprenticed to a renowned Belfast architect called James Hunter.

At the University, Neilson's art is best seen in Pavilions IX and X where he was the master joiner and overseer. He lived in a country house at Keene, in the Green Mountains, where he died in 1827.

Neilson and his two brothers were involved in United Irishman insurgent activity at Ballycarry, their home village near Carrickfergus, County Antrim. William was hanged in his mid-teens, and Samuel and John were banished in 1799 from Ireland. John managed to reach Philadelphia, where he was naturalized and introduced to Thomas Jefferson.[32] He had had connections to prominent UI leaders, and at his death left part of his estate to Mary Ann McCracken, whose brother famed Henry Joy McCracken was hanged in 1798. A "profile" of Neilson was to have been sent to his own wife by way of Roseanna, the widow of stone-cutter John Gorman.

Among Neilson's final effects were his violin/fiddle strings and some two hundred and fifty books. Among his books were some with an Irish dimension: Harsop's *Irish Rebellion*, *A History of Virginia* by fellow United exile John Daly Burk, *MacNeil's Poems, Castle Rackrent, War in Ireland,* and a history of Dublin. In the 1990s a cenotaph was erected to Neilson in the old Maplewood Cemetery in Charlottesville.[33]

It seems safe to conclude that the Irish who were engaged in Jefferson's projects enjoyed their new-found lives free of the weight of English-Irish, loyalist-nationalist history. Dinsmore and Neilson worked as colleagues for some twenty-five years. Being educated men, they must have occasionally chatted about their home county and their families (both were of Presbyterian leanings) and the new world in Virginia. Both did well financially, and owned some slaves. They would probably have known about Antrim man Francis Dinsmore who was imprisoned in 1796 at Carrickfergus for UI membership. According to the *Belfast News-Letter* of 21 October 1796, some three thousand locals turned out "to raise Mr. Francis Dinsmore's potatoes...which they did in six minutes." Most Dinsmores in County Antrim would have been loyal Crown subjects, but then again many of them would have joined (or sympathized with) the UI movement. The principles of enlightenment appealed to many northern Presbyterians, who formed the majority of UI forces in the northeast of Ireland.

When Neilson and Dinsmore were engaged in their work at President Madison's Montpelier estate, they built a small circular Doric temple which rests above a hidden, subterranean ice-house. Their classical training in architecture came to the fore here.

There are ten unfluted columns resting on bases.

The entablature has triglyphs and plain metopes, with guttae below and a dentil molding above the entablature. Both Neilson and Dinsmore probably knew of other circular follies, particularly the Mussenden temple in County Derry, built in 1785, as well as the Federal Edifice in Philadelphia with its thirteen Corinthian columns, built in the same era.

(Readers interested in these Irish artisans are referred to K. Edward Lay's *The Architecture of Jefferson Country*, Richard C. Cote's "The Architectural Workmen of Thomas Jefferson in Virginia", and Peter Hodson's *Birth of a Virginia Plantation House* with its coverage of Neilson and of Bremo House.)

John William Mallet, William Barton Rogers, and John Patten Emmet are three early University professors with Irish connections.

Mallet was born in 1832 near Dublin city, and studied at Trinity College. He taught chemistry at the University for nearly forty years. He was interred in the University cemetery on his death in 1912; Mallet Hall was named in his honor.

William Rogers was born in 1804 in Philadelphia, as was his brother Robert in 1813. Both became science professors at the University. Their scholarly father, Patrick Kerr Rogers, was born in 1776 in Strabane, County Tyrone. Patrick was a political refugee, a United Irishman, who fled to the U.S. for his physical safety. Patrick fiddled and was an avid singer. He taught sciences at William and Mary College until his 1828 death. At the University, Rogers Hall was named for William.

In the University cemetery is buried James Rogers, a native of County Tyrone, "and for fifty years a citizen of the United States," according to his tombstone inscription. He was born circa 1748, and died at the University in 1819 (the same year the University was founded) at age seventy-one. Interestingly enough, in that very year Patrick had applied to the University for a professorship.

John Patten Emmet was born in 1796 in Dublin, where his uncle was to lead an armed insurrection against the English in Ireland: Robert Emmet was executed in 1803, honored in song and story to the present-day. Thomas Jefferson himself invited John

to join the first faculty at the University in 1825 as a professor of sciences. John lived in Pavilion I on the Lawn of the University, where "he kept as pets snakes, a white owl, and a friendly bear."[34] In a few years, he married into the renowned Tucker family, and he and his new wife built a fine two-story brick house called "Morea," which is still in use today.

The bear, alas, was consumed at a celebration for students and faculty.

John Patten Emmet died in 1842, and is interred with other Emmets in New York City. A major

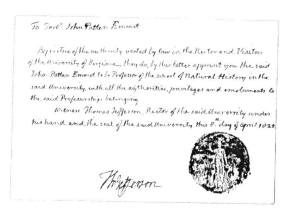

Charlottesville thoroughfare is named Emmet Street; and Emmet House, a dormitory, is named for John. But his young son, John Tucker Emmet, lies today in the University cemetery — a great-nephew of the heroic Robert Emmet.

From the pure regions of eternal joy,
Thou friend of man, delightful Peace! descend;
Then shall ferocious War no more destroy,
But, nations into lasting friendship blend.

—"Peace, An Elegy"

These four lines in iambic pentameter come from the pen of John Corry (1770-1825), born in Ireland near Ravensdale in County Louth. His book, *Odes and elegies, descriptive and sentimental*, was published in Newry Town in 1797. These poems are typical of much eighteenth-century Restoration writing, for nowhere does Corry write in traditional Irish meters or forms. Yet this minor poet is regarded as "sympathetic to republicanism," and further described as "an expatriated Irishman" who moved to England.[35]

A copy of the Corry book appeared in western Albemarle County, and bears the inscription "John Hays, Albemarle 1808". His father, James Hays who died in 1812, "was probably of Irish origin".[36] James had founded a prospective town at the foot of the Blue Ridge Mountains, which was to have carried the name of York or Little York.

It could be argued that the Hays family were simply fond of Enlightenment (Neoclassical) poetry. Perhaps it could be argued equally that the Hays family owned this fairly rare book because they supported an Irish republic and not the English monarchy. *Odes and elegies* [sic] has an obvious political orientation. Among those listed on the page of Subscribers' Names appear a near-dozen United Irish members, all prominent at the time, and many of them to be executed in a few short years: Henry Joy McCracken, Thomas Russell, the Teelings, two Presbyterian divines (Steele Dickson and James Porter), et al.

These endorsements of the poetry collection make clear the UI link to John Corry. A ten-line iambic poem (four lines in tetrameter, six lines in pentameter) has strong UI themes:

The spirit by Dependence broke,
In ignorance must live and die —
Beneath a fellow-mortal's yoke,
Depress'd, he breathes a timid sigh.
But, when Necessity a man compels
To seek subsistence where Abundance dwells,
And serve another's Will for means to live,
His mind, indignant, when Oppression low'rs,
Like Samson, bound with cords, collects his pow'rs,
And rends the trammels that such torment give.

On the title page of Corry's book there is a harp, and the most prominent icon of the UI insurgency movement was the harp encircled by the maxim, "It is new-strung and shall be heard."

Just as the Dinsmore family members in County Antrim were of differing political allegiances, so too the Corry family were of divided views. John and James Corry were cut from a more progressive political cloth than Isaac Corry and his sons who supported the British-imposed Act of Union of 1800. Isaac "informed on" several UI members in the Newry area, and was known locally as "the Traitor". Marcus Corry was serving in 1799 as High Sheriff of County Down.

Among those insurgents executed at Downpatrick Jail in Down was the well-known Thomas Russell, who was hanged and then decapitated. James Corry, a shoe-maker in Downpatrick, was also hanged. Both were fated Subscribers of the *Odes and elegies*.

Russell wrote of the enlightening ideas of the UI program: "We see the vices of the rich in so far from being considered as shameful that some are made honourable. Whence this but from the rich making laws? Property put before life. Property must be altered in some measure."[37]

Although Thomas Jefferson apparently never visited Ireland, for over fifty years he maintained an interest in things Irish. In London in 1769, he purchased two works by Ferdinando Warner published in that decade: *The History of Ireland*, and *The History of the Rebellion and Civil War in Ireland*.

The fact is that Jefferson was extremely well-read. The attention he gave to reading in science, politics, and history was out of the ordinary, even for a figure of the Enlightenment. He gave huge attention to cataloguing the books in his library — and there were over two dozen books pertaining to Ireland [see book list at on Contents page].

Most of these books helped shape Thomas Jefferson's views on Irish culture, and some were extremely important in the formulation of those views. Jefferson had read *Statutes of Ireland in force in 1678*. Among the studies of the eighteenth-century, he owned Sir Henry Cavendish's *Public Accounts of Ireland* (1791), and Sir William Petty's *Political Survey of Ireland* (1719). This latter work originally appeared in 1691 as *The Political Anatomy of Ireland*. In this work Petty calculated that 504,000 Irish people died at the hands of the English, 1642-1653.

Jefferson lent some items from his library to John Daly Burk who wrote *The History of Virginia*, which stretches from the first settlement through the eighteenth century. This four-volume work was published in 1804-05 in Petersburg.

In 1804 Jefferson purchased John Philpot Curran's *Forensic Eloquence: Sketches of Trials in Ireland for High Treason*. Curran was a lawyer who defended United Irishmen in Dublin; he was born in Newmarket, County Cork.

In 1807 Jefferson wrote to thank two Irish radical writers who had each sent him a copy of his book, both of which appeared in print in 1807. UI member James MacNeven wrote *Pieces of Irish History*; and William Sampson wrote his study entitled *Memoirs: including...a short sketch of the history of Ireland*. MacNeven had been exiled to America in 1805; Sampson in 1806. Sampson, like Curran, defended United members in the Irish courts; both of these lawyers carefully avoided UI membership.

Thomas Jefferson possessed a copy of *Bíobla Naomhthan* (The Bible), published 1690 in London. He was also fascinated with, and made constant use of, *The American Gardener's Calendar*, published in Philadelphia in 1806; this gardening book was compiled by the Irish political refugee Bernard McMahon.

A dozen or so letters penned by Jefferson indicate his loathing of the English state and his interest in Ireland. In one missive he asserts, "Great Britain's governing principles are conquest, colonization, commerce, and monopoly." He was writing to William Carmichael in 1790. It is interesting to compare similar thought, diction, and alliterative phrases in John Philpot Curran's writings:

> *The English writers have endeavored to cover the conduct of their government with the cloak of conquest, commerce, and civilization; and, even religion has been brought in to justify injustice, and to sanctify ambition.*[38]

A few months after the British had burned the city of Washington, Thomas Jefferson wrote:

> *We concur in considering the government of England as totally without morality, insolent beyond bearing, inflated with vanity and ambition, aiming at the total dominion of the sea, lost in corruption, of deep-seated hatred towards us, hostile to liberty wherever it endeavors to show its head, and the eternal disturber of the peace of the world.* (In a letter of 1815 to Thomas Leiper.)

Jefferson had shown a kindly mind toward Native Americans in his epistle to Alexander von Humboldt in a letter of 1813:

> *The interested and unprincipled policy of England has defeated all our labors for the salvation of these unfortunate people. They have seduced the greater part of the tribes within our neighborhood, to take up the hatchet against us. ...The confirmed brutalization, if not the extermination of this race in our America, is therefore to*

form an additional chapter in the English history of the same colored man in Asia, and of the brethren of their own color in Ireland, and wherever else Anglo-mercantile cupidity can find a two-penny interest in deluging the earth with human blood.

It might be argued, however, that the most relevant letter about Ireland from Jefferson was sent to James Madison in January of 1799: "Bonaparte... seems to be looking towards the East Indies, where a most formidable cooperation has been prepared for demolishing the British power. **I wish the affairs of Ireland were as hopeful.**" (Emphasis supplied.)

James Monroe and Thomas Jefferson shared a loathing toward the British for several reasons, including the attempt by British troops to capture Jefferson at Monticello in 1781. Jefferson and Monroe had been fellow scholars at William and Mary College, and they "shared lodgings for five months before Jefferson left to serve as American minister to France" in 1784-1789; regarding their time together, "This intimacy seems to have sealed their closeness", ideologically speaking.[39]

Monroe was appointed as U.S. ambassador to France in the years 1794 to 1796, a crucial period in Irish history. In January 1796, Irish revolutionary and activist Wolfe Tone came to Paris, bearing a letter of introduction to James Monroe. As historian David A. Wilson relates, "through Monroe, Tone established the connections with the Directorate that culminated in the invasion attempts of 1796 and 1798" by the French in Ireland.[40] And as another historian, Marianne Elliott, informs us, "In fact Monroe's support was essential to Tone...and Monroe remained a good friend to his mission" to obtain military aid from the French for the armed insurgents of the United Irishmen.[41] Although President George Washington had recalled Monroe in July of 1796, President Jefferson in his first term re-appointed Monroe as Envoy Extraordinary to France in 1803.

Wolfe Tone and his family had been in Philadelphia in 1795, and in the 1790s more than 60,000 Irish fled to the United States, "many of whom left their homeland for political as well as economic reasons."[42] English retaliation for the decade's insurgency had resulted in the deaths of probably 30,000 Irish people.

Jefferson and Monroe met frequently in Philadelphia in 1782, 1797, and 1790. Jefferson hired John Neilson in Philadelphia in 1804 — Neilson, from Ballycarry in County Antrim, was the previously mentioned architect-builder. It was in 1804 that Jefferson had met the distinguished Thomas Addis Emmet and doubtless learned many details of this insurgent family. Jefferson advised Emmet to practice law in New York. Since Emmet was an alien, "he was unqualified. Almost at once [when he arrived] he traveled to Washington, where Jefferson and others told him that his lack of citizenship should not be a disqualification." When Emmet returned to New York he was soon informed by the

Supreme Court that it now "permitted him to practice law despite his alien status."[43]

Thomas Moore was becoming a well-known composer of songs in Ireland, and was a friend of the rebel Robert Emmet during their Trinity College days. Moore came to Virginia in 1803 a few scant months after Robert was executed. He met, among others, Thomas Jefferson and United Irish refugee Thomas Robinson. Jefferson himself wrote a letter of support for Robinson.

It seems reasonable to surmise that Jefferson continued his interest in Irish-English relations beyond the scholarly books he owned and read. Surely he heard grim tales from such political refugees as Thomas Addis Emmett and John Patten Emmet, Thomas Robinson, John Daly Burk, horticulturalist Bernard McMahon, and architect John Neilson. William Sampson became an attorney in New York. There is presently at the University of Washington-Seattle a William Sampson Fellowship, as well as a Thomas Addis Emmet Fellowship, both in Comparative Public Interest Law. William James MacNeven himself became an honored and renowned professor of medicine and physician in New York City.

It also seems reasonable to assume that both President Jefferson and Ambassador Monroe were committed to doing their part in assisting the Irish struggle against the English ruling class and its ferocious soldiery. In return, those in the UI movement who were exiled to North America "did indeed contribute significantly to the democratization of

American life."[44] These exiles campaigned vigorously for Jefferson's election to the presidency, and against the Alien and Sedition laws. As Professor Wilson concludes, "Jefferson established close contacts with radical Irish immigrants, and owed his victory in 1800 at least in part to their organizational and propagandistic skills." [45] It was an era of some transatlantic solidarity. In 1775, during the American battles against the English, "bonfires lit the Antrim skies to celebrate the Battle of Bunker Hill."[46] It is also curious to note, ironically enough, that there is a Bunker Hill in Ireland in a district of County Armagh which is known for its perfervid loyalty to the English crown.

> *When, in the expiring hours of the twentieth century, some chronicler pauses to consider the virtues and deeds of Virginians, he will dwell in loving admiration upon the talents and traits of those of Irish blood, who have already made bricks without straw, and won the confidence and esteem of their neighbors.*
>
> -Joseph T. Lawless, *Journal of the American-Irish Historical Society*, Vol. 2 (1899), p. 165. Secretary of State in Virginia (of Galway parentage)

By the 1770s, only five percent of the land remained in Irish hands,[47] and some had foreseen the horrors of the 1780s and 1790s in Ireland. The early Irish arrivals in the Charlottesville area found niches for themselves as builders, grocers, architects, plasterers, printers, stonemasons, carriage-makers, or portrait painters. In short, they were able to use their acquired skills, they were literate, and they were becoming part of the middle class.

By contrast, there were two thousand or so impoverished Irish who swept into the Charlottes-ville-to-Staunton area in the decades 1820 to 1860. The majority used Irish (or Gaelic) as their primary language. They had barely eked out a precarious year-by-year existence as tenants on the land that their ancestors had once owned.

These new Irish arrivals (male, by and large) desperately needed the work they fell into as workers on Virginia canals, roads, and railways. Many of them were known in Ireland as spalpeens, or wandering farm workers.

Most of these Irish came from County Cork, but others came from Kerry, Tipperary, Limerick, and Galway. The cataclysm of *An Gorta Mór* (the Great Hunger, also called the Famine) was the primary compelling force behind their emigrating between 1845 and 1855. Overall, at least one million Irish died from starvation or linked diseases. Another two million fled, primarily to North America (including some five thousand to Virginia). About a half million were evicted from their humble Irish homes.

In County Cork alone, an estimated 150,000 deaths stemmed from the Hunger era. In Cork City there were hundreds of cholera deaths. Some 50,000 managed to emigrate from Cork to the US and Canada.

Construction of the Blue Ridge Railroad in Virginia in the 1850s was an immense project. The most difficult aspect was the building of the four tunnels, around which Irish shanties and slave quarters developed. These tunnels from east to west were named the Greenwood, Brooksville, Rock or Short, and the long Crozet or Blue Ridge tunnel, which was over 4,000 feet in length. The work was physically demanding, from heaving picks to hammering metal drills, from loading the debris of boulders and earth into horse-pulled wagons, and to laying the iron rails.

(The curious reader is directed to the website www.ClannMhor.org. Workers' names are contained in a sizable spreadsheet under the heading of RESEARCH.)

Most of the Blue Ridge workers had come from County Cork, and smaller numbers from Kerry, Tipperary, Galway, Clare, and Limerick. Many of their names are contained in payroll records available at the Library of Virginia in Richmond. These Irish are also cited in birth, marriage, and death records for the counties of Augusta, Nelson, and Albemarle. Some of them applied for citizenship during their Virginia work years. Many were married by Father Daniel Downey, pastor of St. Francis of Assisi church in nearby Staunton town; many were later interred at Thornrose Cemetery in that town.

Many of these workers had labored on Maryland railway construction, work contracted out to John Kelly and John Larguey. Some may have been involved in Virginia canal-building efforts, and doubtless some had worked on road/turnpike projects.

The rail line was to stretch overall from Richmond through the Blue Ridge Mountains to Cincinnati and ultimately to Chicago. Most of the Irish workers continued with this undertaking; few of them seemed to have stayed in Virginia. Some two hundred died during the years of tunnel construction, the causes being accidents, exhaustion, and the cholera. At least two slaves died during this era.

The Irish and the slave workers accomplished a phenomenal feat on the seventeen-mile Blue Ridge Railroad stretch, and this work reflected obvious class struggle. The Irish emigrant had been the *íochtarán*, the underdog, the oppressed man in Ireland; he was much on a par with the African-American slave. By contrast the French civil engineer Claudius Crozet, the director of this railway project, did well socially and financially, as did the master contractor, John Kelly.

It is well to note elements in a lengthy letter that appeared in *The Cork Examiner* in 1860. The writer was one Michael Adams, Irish-born, who had spent twelve years on Virginia's railways. He had come to live at Sweet Springs community in Monroe County (west of the Blue Ridge tunnels).

> *Such is the condition of the Irish railroad labourer...it is indescribable; it would take more than a mere letter to tell you the despicable, humiliating, slavish life*

of an Irish labourer on a railroad in the States; I believe I can come very near it by saying that everything, good and bad, black and white, is against him; no love for him-no protection in life-can be shot down, run through, kicked, cuffed, spat on-and no redress, but a response of served the damn son of an Irish b-------right, damn him.

My concluding advice is, if people will come to America having nothing definite in view, let their pursuit be after a piece of land somewhere, anywhere-anything but public works or living in cities.

Those Irish who arrived in Virginia to build the railway would have known (directly or indirectly) of "rural disturbances," a mild expression from the English administration. During the 1820s and beyond, the military stepped in to repress agrarian confrontations, particularly in County Cork but also in adjacent counties. The rural guerillas were variously called Rockites (allies of a "Captain Rock") or Ribbonmen or Whiteshirts. Of those arrested by the English military or the police, more than one hundred were executed for so-called "Rockite crimes". Irish protestors were struggling over grazing rights, rising rents, maltreatment by landlords, and tithes demanded by the foreign church (Anglican, or Church of Ireland). In short, what historian Thomas Bartlett defines as class divisions and class objectives. The hostilities stemmed therefore from defense of the rights of the native Irish poor. The result of the Act of Union (passed by the English parliament in 1800) was "alienation rather than integration" of the Irish population.[48] As Bartlett assures us, Ireland had in the early 1800s "an intensely politicized peasantry."[49]

In light of the devastating first years of the Hunger, small wonder that the immense emigration movement out of Ireland happened. The fears of those in Cork and other counties were prescient and well-founded. As economist Joel Mokyr observed, "most serious of all, when the chips were down in the frightful summer of 1847, the British simply abandoned the Irish and let them perish."[50]

From the 1700s, it was seen as an obligation of the British government to provide relief during difficult agricultural and famine periods. Yet, as Belfast historian Peter Gray points out, Parliament provided "less than half of one percent of the British gross national product"[51] during the worst five years of the Hunger. Gray's assessment echoes that of economist Mokyr. Gray concludes, "That more was not in fact spent on keeping people alive was due to the triumph of ideological obsession over humanitarianism."[52]

Endnotes

1. Edward Woods, *Albemarle County in Virginia* (1901), p. 53.
2. Woods, p. 258.
3. Woods, p. 68
4. James Alexander, *Early Charlottesville: Recollections of James Alexander* (1963), ed. Mary Rawlings, p. 56.
5. K. Edward Lay, *The Architecture of Jefferson Country* (2000), p. 194.
6. Richard Guy Wilson, *The Builders and Workers of Thomas Jefferson's Academical Village* (2009). Website.
7. Robert C. Fitzgerald, *My Roots in Nelson County, Virginia* (1999), p.28.
8. Michael J. O'Brien, "Extracts from Virginia Church Records," *Journal of the American-Irish Historical Society 18* (1919), pp. 205-207.
9. *Nelson County Virginia Heritage* (2001), p. 120.
10. Lay, p. 136. Includes photograph of the Butler House.
11. Margaret Fowler Clark, "Correspondence and Notes re: Butler, Fowler, and Staples Families," University of Virginia Special Collections, access number 4702-e.
12. Woods, pp. 339-340.
13. Alexander, p. 81.
14. Alexander, p. 20.
15. Alexander, p. 95.
16. Alexander, p. 57.
17. Woods, p. 70.
18. Alexander, pp. 102-103.
19. Alexander, p. 117.
20. Alexander, p. 105.
21. *Central Gazette*, December 25th, 1824.
22. Rosamond Jacob, *The Rise of the United Irishmen* (1937), p. 253.
23. Charles Dickson, *The Wexford Rising in 1798: Its Causes and Its Course* (1956), p. 173.
24. William B. Coles, *The Coles Family of Virginia* (1989), p. 5.
25. Coles, p. 26.
26. Coles, p. 116.
27. Lay, p. 104.
28. Lay, p. 104.

29. Lay, pp. 103-104.
30. Lay, p. 101.
31. *Magazine of Albemarle Charlottesville History 46* (1988).
32. Richard R. Madden, *The United Irishmen: Their Lives and Times* (Dublin, 1858, 2nd Series, four volumes), Vol. 1, pp. 336-338.
33. Kevin Donleavy, *Dedication of the Monument to John Neilson* (1999). Twelve pages.
34. Harry Clemons, *Notes on the Professors...*, p.33.
35. John Corry, "Odes and Elegies". Internet commentary.
36. Electronic communication from Sam Towler, July 20th, 2010.
37. J.W. Boyle, ed., *Leaders and Workers* (Cork, 1966), p. 87.
38. *Speeches of John Philpot Curran* (New York, Vol. 1, 1811), pp. 28-29.
39. Noble E. Cunningham, Jr., *Jefferson and Monroe — Constant Friendship and Respect* (2003), p. 10.
40. David A. Wilson, *United Irishmen, United States* (1998), p. 154.
41. Marianne Elliott, *Wolfe Tone: Prophet of Irish Independence* (1989), p. 287.
42. Wilson, p. 2.
43. Michael Durey, in *Artisans, Peasants and Proletarians* (ed. Clive Emsley, 1985), pp. 184-185.
44. Wilson, p. 2.
45. Wilson, p. 2.
46. Wilson, p. 14.
47. *Cork Examiner*, August 10th , 1860.
48. Thomas Bartlett, *Ireland — A History* (2010), p. 262.
49. Bartlett, cited in *A Millstreet Miscellany*: Shunsuke Katsuta, "The Rockite Movement in County Cork in the Early 1820s," 24-42, p. 37.
50. John Crowley et al., eds., *Atlas of the Great Irish Famine* (2012), p. 63.
51. Peter Gray, *The Irish Famine* (1995). pp. 94-95.
52. Gray, p. 95.

CHAPTER 7

Lynchburg and the Counties of Amherst, Bedford, Campbell, and Rockbridge

*N*orfolk and Winchester had an Irish presence in the late 1700s, as we have seen. There was also an Irish element in the area which was to become the town of Lynchburg: in the counties of Amherst, Bedford, Campbell, and Rockbridge.

Marriage records reveal names of some Irish residents in Amherst:

John Lonegan married Elizabeth Stratton in 1798.
Benjamin Kelley married Nancy Jarrell in 1790.
Elizabeth Moran married John Bolling in 1793.
John Phelan married Salley Haines in 1793.
Edmund Coffey married Tildy Fitzgerald in 1798.
James Gahagan married Elizabeth Murrell in 1798.

These marriages were followed by more in the 1800s. In 1800 Jane Fitzpatrick married; in 1811 Lucindy Doyle married; in 1812 Catherine Doyle married; in 1814 James Fitzpatrick married; and in 1811 John Brady married.

In 1782, part of Bedford County became the

new Campbell County. In that same year, Charles Lynch Jr. was sworn in as a justice of the Campbell County court. John Fitzpatrick was appointed also as a justice. Local Campbell archives include these Irish marriages:

> *In 1793, Henry Cane married Sarah Stevens.*
> *In 1804, Dennis Kelley married Mary Strange.*
> *In 1807, Jeremiah Keen married Patsy Mooman.*
> *In 1800, Polly Shannon married Edward McCawley.*
> *In 1796, Edward Lynch married Polly Terrell.*
> *In 1789, Sally Lynch married Charles Terrell. (She was the daughter of Charles Lynch Sr.)*

Some early area residents had been born in the 1700s. They emigrated from many different places in Ireland; there was no sizable contingent from any one place.

> *James Duffel was born in 1759 in Derry city.*
> *Twins James and Dan McCarty were born circa 1793 in Cork.*
> *Ducre Kinnier was born in 1797 in County Monaghan.*
> *John Kinnier (Ducre's husband) was born 1795 in Castleblaney, County Monaghan.*
> *Bernard Finney was born circa 1797 in Leitrim.*
> *John Kyle was born circa 1798 in Tyrone.*
> *James Dolan was born circa 1798 in Dublin.*
> *Mary Dolan (James' wife) was born circa 1770 in Dublin.*
> *William Dornin was born in 1782 in County*

Antrim.
John Liggat was born circa 1772 in County Antrim.
Michael Connell was born in 1794 in Prosperous, County Kildare.
Eugene McCarthy was born in 1799 in Kerry.
James Cunningham was born in 1798 in Roscommon.
James Victor Knight was born in 1797 in Stewartstown, County Tyrone.
Dan Boyle was born in 1795 in County Monaghan.
Anne Boyle (Dan's wife) was born circa 1775.
James Clark was born circa 1798.
Michael Fox was born circa 1793.
James Boal was born circa 1798.
Moses Ross was born circa 1797.
Sinnamond Noble was born circa 1795 [Noble Cinnamond ?].
Richard Halpen was born in 1795.
Richard H. Burks was born circa 1767.
Mrs. Nancy Fitzgerald was born in 1792.
Charles Hoyle was born in 1750.
Robert Forsythe was born in 1794.

Other Lynchburg men born in the 1700s fought in the War of 1812; among them were William Lynch, Peter Daugherty, and William Doyle.

Five newish Lynchburg arrivals made early applications for citizenship: James Wade in 1822, George Hoyle in 1821, Michael Fox in 1818, James Boal in 1821, and Sinnamond Noble in 1818. (More details concerning citizenship applications will appear later in this chapter.)

Another indicator of the Irish in Lynchburg is the recording of some scant details of children's deaths:

> *Adeline, daughter of James G. and Mary E. Swinney, died in 1818 at age 7.*
> *Ellen, daughter of James Treacy of County Cork, died in 1838, only 11 months of age.*
> *Thomas died age 11 months, whose father was John Sheehan of Dunscale, County Kerry.*
> *Cynthia Fitzpatrick died as an infant, year unknown.*
> *Infant John P. Bowles died in 1850; infant Francis Bowles in 1852. Their parents Patrick and Catherine had emigrated from Riverstown, County Sligo.*
> *James died age 12 months, son of Patrick Griffen from County Kerry.*

The saga of one family is of prime importance to Lynchburg. Charles Lynch was a fifteen-year-old Catholic youth when he left Galway about 1720. He became indentured to a Virginia Quaker family, the Clarks; he eventually married Sarah Clark in 1733. Her father Christopher had become a prominent land-speculator east of Charlottesville, in the area of present-day estates Coolyn, Bridle Spur, and Tall Oaks. Charles himself "became the leading real estate dealer in early Albemarle," having learned from Christopher Clark's expertise.[1] Charles eventually owned some 6,500 acres in Albemarle's Pen Park area. The Clark and Lynch families were slave owners.

Charles and Sarah built Chestnut Hill estate in Campbell County overlooking the James River shortly before his 1753 death. He had represented Albemarle County in the House of Burgesses, and had been an Albemarle justice a few years prior to that. Tradition says this Irishman is interred on Chestnut Hill land.

Among the Lynch offspring were Charles Jr. (born 1736) and John (born 1740) and two daughters. The young Charles was known for his loathing of the English and their supporters in Virginia. He became a colonel in the Revolutionary War era, and was elected to the House of Delegates.

John Lynch is considered the founder of Lynchburg. He donated some Lynch family land to establish the town. There is a commemorative boulder set beside the James River today, which bears a bronze plaque lauding John's local contributions. The stone marks the site of the John Lynch ferry across the river. Their father Charles had owned the Rivanna River ferry in the Charlottesville area. John is buried in the graveyard beside the Quaker Meeting House in Lynchburg, his death occurring in 1820.

(Thanks to Charlottesville resident Maggie Wilson for many details of the Clark-Lynch nexus.)

There are several Irish-oriented venues between Charlottesville and Lynchburg. Keene is a tiny crossroads below Charlottesville on Route 20, in the Green Mountain section. Its name derives from

Robert G. H. Kean, who was a Lynchburg attorney at one time. Born in 1828 in Virginia, he married in 1854 the celebrated Jane Randolph, daughter of Thomas Jefferson Randolph, kinsman of President Jefferson. The couple lived for some time at Keene. Kean was city attorney in Lynchburg; he is buried at Spring Hill cemetery, his wife in the Monticello graveyard.

The are two conflicting stories regarding the origin of this Kean family. Kean's son believed that his great-grandfather was one Samuel Kean, who emigrated in 1760 to America from County Armagh. Another source indicates the great-grandfather was Dr. Andrew Kean, educated at Trinity College Dublin before coming to the States.[2]

There are other Irish links to the Keene district. John Neilson, architect-builder and United Irishmen militant had a house at Keene which he called Refuge. Another link is the nearby Enniscorthy estate, which was designed and built by another Irishman, James Dinsmore. (The reader is urged to refer to the Charlottesville chapter for more details about Neilson and Dinsmore.)

There is a small community called Kelly, some five miles east of Lynchburg on Route 460. There were Kellys here at least as early as the 1840s, and there is a small Kelly cemetery as well.

Just north of Lynchburg is Athlone on Route 674. Most of the house was built between 1780 and 1840, but an earlier section went up in about 1732. A 1759 deed book of Amherst County indicates that Irish-born Thomas Clark was an early owner of Athlone. (A photograph of the house appears in Farrar and Hines, *Old Virginia Houses — The Piedmont*. These editors mention that the house was named after the town in Ireland.)

Next to Athlone is the community of Canody's Store (cf. Kennedy).

Three counties meet at the Irish Creek area: Amherst, Nelson, and Rockbridge. In 1846, tin was being mined at Irish Creek. Iron mines were in use at Little Irish Creek about 1900.

There are several hundred Irish interred in Lynchburg at Presbyterian Cemetery, Old City Cemetery, and Holy Cross Cemetery. Old City was opened in 1806, on land donated by John Lynch. Presbyterian was established in 1823. The first burials at Holy Cross took place in 1875. (This cemetery is also known as St. Francis Xavier.)

Among the surnames at Old City and Presbyterian graveyards are Dolan, Donahoe, Dornin, Dowdy, Dulaney, Gallagher, Garaghty, Hogan, Kelly, and Maloney, inter alia. Their roots were in counties Cork, Kerry, Monaghan, Roscommon, and Sligo.

More than one one hundred Irish burials in Holy Cross Cemetery attest to the greater number of Irish counties represented, some fifteen or so, including Clare, Cork, Galway, Kerry, Kilkenny, Limerick, Longford, Meath, Monaghan, Roscommon, Sligo, Tipperary, Tyrone, Wexford, and Wicklow.

Charles Hoyle is interred at Old City graveyard. He was cited as "an excellent and venerable man," and a native of Ireland, "where he occupied a high standing among the Irish gentry." However, "He found it expedient to emigrate to America, and settled in Lynchburg."³ Hoyle lived from 1750 to 1825. His inscription strongly suggests he was a political refugee, fleeing the cruel military repression during the 1798 Rising.

Among the many well-carved headstones at Holy Cross is this inscription: BORN IN SWEET COUNTY CLARE, IRELAND. The stone marks the grave of Patrick J. O'Halloran, 1820 to 1905.

One of the more interesting names of the dead in Presbyterian Cemetery is Robert Emmet Rodes (1829-1864). His name honors the heroic Robert Emmet, hanged in 1803 in Dublin for leading the insurrection against British rule. Rodes served in the Confederate army as a major general; there is an American fiddle tune named for him, "Rodes's Division".

In the Old City Cemetery lie the remains of Briget McGrath Cannaday. She lived from 1802 to 1850 near the newly-dug canal, and she died in a landslide while living at the foot of a bluff.

Holy Cross burials include Monaghan individuals named McGurk, Rooney, McCarron, McMahon, and McDivitt. There are such Cork and Kerry surnames as Donovan, Moriarty, Sullivan, Spillane, Harragan, Desmond, and Gregory. Michael Lawless came from Meath, and the McSorleys came from Tyrone. Thomas Ryan emigrated from Tipperary, as did some O'Gormans. There are some Byrnes from Wicklow, as well as Gilfoyles from Kilkenny.

Many of Lynchburg's Irish families have continued to live there. The 1902 Register for Holy Cross School's young budding scholars contains some forty Irish surnames, such as Dunn, Hurley, Hanafin, Mallan, Lawless, O'Halloran, Doyle, Sullivan, Cahill, Driscoll, Spillane, O'Meara, and the like.

The history of the Catholic church in Lynchburg dates back to 1843. The construction of the Kanawha Canal in 1834 contributed to its growth. Thousands of Irish Catholics were employed for the project, and many workers established their families in or near Lynchburg after the completion of the canal. A building located at Ninth and Clay streets was acquired in 1843 for use as the first church, named St. Francis Xavier. (Website for Holy Cross Catholic School)

Irish stone-cutters seemingly were in high demand in these Virginia counties in the 1800s. They were crucial to carving granite blocks for canal locks, and later (1850s) chiseling stone for railway culverts and tunnels (see the Charlottesville chapter).

In the 1850 census for Bedford County, there were nine "stonies" enumerated. Stone-cutters were Robert Foyle, age 25, and John Long, age 50. Those calling themselves stonemasons were Michael Gleeson, age 27; Tom McGarvin, 45; Felix Riely, 27; Robert Logan, 25; Michael Trainer, 33; James Mulby, 26; James Warder, 26; and Lawrence

Byrne, who arrived in 1848. He and his brother John had emigrated from County Wicklow.

The Lynchburg town census of 1850 includes these stonemasons: William Murphy, who was 30, John Riley, age 45, Patrick Casey, age 30, and Phil Duffy, age 35. Also in Lynchburg was one of the numerous Fagans, George Fagan, a 28-year-old marble-cutter.

In the 1860 Lexington census, two stone-cutters appeared, Archibald Fagan (30) and Richard Johnson (48). A Lexington stonemason was one Patrick H. Donnelly, who lived from 1790 to 1840.

In Campbell County's 1850 census, stonemason Thomas Garrety [Garraghty] received his US citizenship in 1844. Born circa 1815, he died in 1887. Another stonemason was Richard Halpen, born about 1795.

The Fagan family members were well-known in Lynchburg, Lexington, Salem, and Liberty. George, born about 1815; James, born 1825; Ambrose, born 1829; and Archibald, born 1830, referred to themselves as both marble sculptors and stone-cutters. In the immense Old City Cemetery in Lynchburg, some 46 white marble headstones were carved by George and James, for both black and white deceased.[4] The Fagans, said to be natives of County Carlow, seem to have plied their skills in Philadelphia before they moved to Virginia.

(Today, there is a well-known stone business, the Carlow Stone Center, in Ballykealy. There is a book written by Michael Conry, *Carlow Granite: Years of History Written in Stone* (2006). In Carlow, there are stone townhouses with granite entablatures, Doric porticos, turrets, and mullioned windows, all carved of stone. In Carlow town itself, there are the all-granite courthouse and jail.)

There are several pertinent stories about early Irish individuals in Lynchburg. The first Mass was conducted by Father Daniel Downey (from Downpatrick in County Down) in 1829 at the home of the Dornins. William Dornin was from County Antrim. He was a 68-year-old tobacconist, and his wife Mary (born in New York) was age 49 (census of 1850).

Their daughter Constance Dornin married Patrick Quinn in 1841. Two years later, Patrick was elected secretary of the local Repeal group:

"One important meeting, most appropriate for this day, occurred on the Fourth of July [1843]; the object was to organize a Repeal of the Union Association. In 1801, England had by bribery and other forms of corruption destroyed the Irish Parliament and had incorporated it with her own. Against this crime Irishmen rose in protest from every quarter of the globe where English tyranny had driven them."[5]

An addendum comes from a local cemetery study, *Behind the Old Brick Wall*, in which we learn more about this Repeal group in Lynchburg:

"The Irish citizens, though far away, had not forgotten the Emerald Isle... The Association continued for some time and did much good, by raising money and by creating a sentiment for the oppressed."[6]

The year 1869 saw a new Lynchburg group formed, the Total Abstinence Beneficial Society. The officers elected were Patrick McDivitt, James O'Brien, John Casey, Patrick Doherty, John Kelly, and the Reverend Father J. J. McGurk.[7]

At the Jones Memorial Library there is a database of nearly 400 names of Irish people who made their declaration for US citizenship between 1810 and 1865 in Lynchburg. This library listing includes 58 emigres from Cork, 30 from Kerry, 20 from Monaghan, 9 from Tyrone, and smaller numbers from other counties. There were only some nine individuals declaring in the 1830s. The figure swelled to 73 in the 1840s, and even higher to 290 in the 1850s, as fear, hunger, and terror drove increasing numbers of Irish people from their homeland.

Among those who applied for citizenship was Martin O'Meara, born in Tipperary in 1816. He became a citizen in 1853. By the 1850 Lynchburg census, he and his wife Catherine (nee Smith) had four children, John, Margaret, Tom, and Joe. Martin died in 1891, and is interred at Holy Cross Cemetery. He was described as "an old and honored Irish citizen."[8]

Another who declared his citizenship intention was the Patrick Quinn previously mentioned. He was born in County Tyrone in 1817, and became a US citizen in 1844.

Other Irish applicants: Michael Connell was a local merchant, age 54 in 1850, living with his Irish-born wife Mary (age 60). James Cunningham was a grocer, born about 1799. Father Daniel Downey himself received his citizenship papers in 1849, as did Michael Day, a laborer aged 36. Charles McCarty, born 1810, was a worker on the Lynchburg stretch of the James River and Kanawha Canal in 1851. Michael Murphy was listed as "Rope Maker" in the census, having been born about 1817. James Wrenn, born circa 1820, was described as "Shoemaker" in the census, and his age was listed as 20.

In the mid-eighteen hundreds an influx of willing-to-work Irish filled the ranks of those constructing roads and turnpikes, canals, and rail lines. Some 400 were enumerated in the Bedford County census of 1850. Two described themselves as contractors, Patrick Gunn and John McQuade. Dennis O'Sullivan was a 30-year-old boot maker.

In this period, the Bedford court conferred citizenship on at least nine Irish males: John Barrett, Richard Barrett, John Crotty, Tim Driscoll, Simon Donohoe, Pierce Kilmartin, James McCormack, Phil Murray, and James Ryan.[9] Among the early Bedford area arrivals Stephen Goggin came about 1742 with his family.

As for George Canady, his father John was born in 1717: his mother was Margaret Rowan, born in 1719. George was born in Bedford County in 1747; ultimately he and wife Sarah (nee Witt) farmed some seventy acres in the county.

There is a political saga attached to the Byrne brothers in Bedford County:

Lawrence Byrne came to the U.S.A. from Wicklow, Ireland, in 1848, as did his brother John. They owned 1500 sheep in the mountains of Wicklow near the village of Seven Churches. They sold the sheep for $1.00 each, and went off to join the "young Irish" in the 1848 "rising" against British rule. The "rising of 48" was a disaster. Lawrence and John, fearing British retributions, fled to this country with $750 each in cash.[10]

Lawrence was also a stonemason. He subcontracted in culvert-building in Virginia for the fore-runner of the Norfolk and Western Railroad. Lawrence was known to be opposed to slavery in America. He married Ellen Kelly who was an emigrant from Dublin. They farmed near Lowry in Bedford. He was Lowry postmaster at one point and helped build the first Catholic church in Bedford.

There were more than 380 Irish-born cited in the Botetourt County census of 1850. The youngest of those listed were Edward Bregan (18) and Pat Brittle (18), John Curry (17), and William Steel (18). Most of the other Irish were in their twenties and thirties. The county labor force included at least five stonemasons: Patrick Faha (cf. Fahey), Thomas Casey, James Muley, Michael McDonald, and Jeremy Carey. Listed as stone-cutters were

Andy Conner, John King, Tom Dowd, William Welch, Michael Flannagan, Edward Hanley, James Hanley, and Nicholas Duffey.

Of the several canal-building projects in Virginia, the James River and Kanawha Canal is the longest at 196 miles. It stretched from Richmond to Buchanan. Initial work began in 1835, and by 1840 the stretch of some 146 miles was completed between Richmond and Lynchburg. Travel time by boat between these two towns was thirty-three hours.

Passenger and goods traffic made use primarily of the James River. Where sections of rough water through rocks were encountered, canal sections were constructed and water in the locks lifted the boats. Some ninety locks, and well over 100 bridges, were built over the entire length. Irish stone-carvers and stonemasons did much of this work. Documents indicate Irish presence along the James River: Foley's Island, Ireland Ford, Downey community, and Feagan's Island.

In the 1880s, the canal went out of use, having been made redundant by the growth of Virginia's railways. Yet in the 1830s and later, there were some 2,000 Irish and 1,000 slaves engaged in the work on the JR&K Canal.

There was an earlier canal built on the James River from 1824 to 1828. Labeled the Blue Ridge Canal, it was built to bypass Balcony Falls some miles past Lynchburg. There were Irish workers here, as evidenced by notes written by civil engineer

Claudius Crozet, who cited Irish Falls and St. Patrick's Rock on the river.

The names of a few Blue Ridge Canal workers are recorded: John Murphy, Patrick Kelly, and John Edwards. These three applied in Lynchburg for citizenship in the 1840s and 1850s. Three other BR Canal workers died in 1825, apparently from cholera, and they are interred on a hillside near the canal. James Clark was born in Ireland about 1798; Thomas Wylie from County Antrim was born about 1800; and James McClarty of Ayrshire (sic) Scotland was born about 1797.

"Next to nothing is known about the thousands of laborers, primarily African-Americans and Irishmen, who toiled and suffered and died in anonymity. The exploitation of these groups was fearful. Servitude and desperation forced them into lives that were Hell on Earth. We can use our imaginations to come up with how intolerable their existences were: the shanty camps in the miasmic river lowlands, the grueling dawn-to-dusk labor in muck, the sickness, the inadequate diet, and above all, the lack of hope."[11]

The work situation was as grim for canalers as for the rail hands of the 1850s, whether Irish or slave workers.

> While hiring out slave labor might have been a great deal for plantation owners, it was one of the worst things that could have happened for the slaves....Slaves could also be worked harder, and there was no need to negotiate the niceties of pay, food, or shelter.[12]

A slave owner did not want a slave to die from being overworked, a financial loss of $1,000 or more for the owner. Irish workers were disposable, cheap, and easily forgotten if they met an early demise.

> *It is needless to speak of the intense heat of the season, or to say that it exceeded anything in the memory of the oldest men. In the early part of July [1838], some 15 or 20 of the Irishmen suddenly expired under the intensity of the heat. Between 100 and 200 of their countrymen left the work and moved north.[13]*

In the words of a modern commentator, we can see more of the parallel between Irish and Black people. He decries the

> *racist British attitude which placed the*

*Irishman and the Negro at the bottom of
a human scale which began just above the
ape.*[14]

The respected American historian Richard Dunn
comments on the human side of Black people:

*The most tragic thing about Afro-American
slavery is that all the black man's
admirable human qualities—his sociability,
adaptability, endurance, loving kindness,
and domesticated disciplined culture—
earned him nothing but debasement in the
New World.*[15]

A slave owner in America could not understand
his slaves' native language. He considered it crude,
barbaric, unimportant. In like manner, an English
plantation owner (as well as an American rail boss)
thought along similar lines, that Irish culture and
language were manifestations of an inferior race.
These planters and entrepreneurs were unaware
of, for example, the contributions of Irish scholars
and clerics who spread learning across Europe
in medieval times. They could not see the marks
of Greek and Roman classical erudition in the
following verse from the sixteenth century:

*Sad to fare from the hills of Fál,
Sad to leave the land of Ireland!
The sweet land of the bee-haunted bens,
Isle of the hoof-prints of young horses.*[16]

Irish and slave labor was the building element on other Virginia projects, as well: the Rivanna River canal of the late 1700s, the Rappahannock canal, the Danville canal, and the Chesapeake & Albemarle canal.

Around the US, the era of the canalers was highly visible. In the Maryland and Washington DC area, there was the C&O canal along the Potomac River. The Erie Canal was constructed, some 300 miles in length. There were Irish workers building Ohio, Pennsylvania, and Illinois and Michigan canals. (On the latter, there were more than 800 Irish fatalities from malaria, rattlesnakes, cholera, and typhus.) In Louisiana, estimates of the mostly Irish canal deaths range from 8,000 to 20,000, a very grim statistic.

In Ireland, there was a spate of canal-building, too. The Newry Canal was the first, in 1731. There were the immensely long Royal and Grand canals of the late 1700s and early 1800s. The Ulster (northern) Canal was opened in 1841. By comparison, the first rail lines in Ireland were built in the 1830s-1840s period.

As a memorial to the many thousand Irish who built the infrastructure of canals, roads, and railways in the US, let the following names of canalers be emblematic of all their fellow-workers. These were the 1851 canal hands laboring on the JR&K canal above Lynchburg:

James Bowles
Owen Callahan
Bart. Connell
William Connell
Simon Crowley
Ambrose Hayden
William Hurley
John Leahy
Timothy Long
Michael Lynch
Thomas Mackey
Charles McCarty
Michael Moran

Eugene Callahan
Martin Casey
Patrick Connell
Jerry Connor
Patrick Cunningham
Patrick Hayden
John Hynes
Daniel Long
Cornelius Lynch
Patrick Lynch
Thomas Mahan
Dan Meagher

(Thanks to the following researchers of Lynchburg history: Douglas MacLeod, Janet Hahn, Bill Trout, Ted Delaney, Wayne Rhodes, and Tim Small. Finally, curious readers are directed to *The Tiller*, which is the journal of the Virginia Canals and Navigations Society.)

Endnotes

1. Jay Worrall, Jr., "The Albemarle Quakers, 1742-1754," in *Magazine of Albemarle County History*, Vol. 40 (pp. 25-44), p. 29.
2. Rosa Faulkner Yancey, *Lynchburg and Its Neighbors* (Richmond: Ferguson, 1935), p. 349.
3. Evelyn Moore and Lucy Baber, *Behind the Old Brick Wall* (Lynchburg: Warwick House, 1998), p. 56. Original edition, 1968.
4. According to the research by Ted Delaney, Old City archivist.
5. Grace Walsh, *The Catholic Church in Lynchburg 1829-1936* (Lynchburg: Coleman & Bradley, 1936), p. 14.
6. Moore & Baber, p. 133.
7. Moore & Baber, p. 295.
8. Moore & Baber, p. 393.
9. Bedford County Order Books, #27-33.
10. *Bedford Heritage*, p. 83.
11. Langhorne Gibson, *Cabell's Canal: The Story of the James River and Kanawha Canal* (Richmond: Commodore Press, 2000), pp. 5-6.
12. Gary Robertson, columnist in the *Richmond Times-Dispatch*, June 26, 1999.
13. Joseph Cabell, annual JR&KC report, December, 1838.
14. Alf MacLochlainn, "Gael and Peasant — A Case of Mistaken Identity?" (pp. 17-36), in Daniel J. Casey and Robert E. Rhodes, eds., *Views of the Irish Peasantry 1800-1916* (Hamden, Connecticut: Archon, 1977), p. 23.
15. Richard S. Dunn, *Sugar and Slaves: The Rise of the Planter Class in the English West Indies, 1624-1713* (New York: Norton, 1973), p. 74.
16. Gerald Nugent, "A Farewell to Fál" (translated by Padraic Pearse), in Kathleen Hoagland, *1000 Years of Irish Poetry* (Old Greenwich, Connecticut: Devin-Adair, 1947), p. 148.

Thomas Jefferson's Books Pertaining to Irish Matters

Baxter, John. *A New and Impartial History of England...Together with every Remarkable Transaction respecting Ireland and other Countries.* London, circa 1796.

Biobla Naomhtha. London, 1690.

Burk, John Daly. *The History of Virginia, from its first settlement to the present day.* Petersburg, Virginia, 1804-5.

Caldwell, Sir James. *Debates relative to the affairs of Ireland; in the years 1763 and 1764.* London, 1766.

Cavendish, Sir Henry. *Cavendish's Public Accounts of Ireland.* London, 1791.

Curran, John Philpot. *Forensic Eloquence: Sketches of Trials in Ireland for High Treason, etc, including the Speeches of Mr. Curran at length: accompanied by certain papers illustrating the history & present state of that country.* Baltimore, 1804. [Jefferson purchased his copy in 1804.]

Dalrymple, Sir John. *Memoirs of Great Britain and Ireland, 1681-1692.* Dublin, 1771.

De Lolme, Jean Louis. *An Essay, containing a few strictures on the Union of Scotland with England; and on the present situation of Ireland.* London, 1787.

Grattan, Henry. *Present State of Ireland.* Philadelphia, 1797.

Kimber, Edward. *The Peerage of Ireland*. London, 1768.

MacNeven, James. *Pieces of Irish History, illustrative of the Condition of the Catholics of Ireland, of the Origin and Process of the Political System of the United Irishmen; and of their Transactions with the Anglo-Irish Government*. New York, 1807.

McMahon, Bernard. *The American Gardener's Calendar*. Philadelphia, 1806.

Molyneux, William. *The Case of Ireland's Being Bound by the Acts of Parliament in England, Stated*. Dublin, 1776. [Original edition, 1698.]

Moore, Thomas. *A Selection of Irish Melodies*. Philadelphia, 1808.

O'Brien, Sir Lucius Henry. *Letters Concerning the Trade & Manufactures of Ireland*. Dublin [?], 1785.

O'Bryen, Dennis. *Utrum Horum? The Government; or, the Country?* Dublin, 1796.

O'Connor, Arthur. *Address to the free electors of the County of Antrim*. Philadelphia, 1792; Dublin, 1796.

O'Connor, Arthur. *Etat actuel de la Grande-Bretagne*. Paris, 1804.

Petty, Sir William. *Political Survey of Ireland*. London, 1719. [Originally published as *The Political Anatomy of Ireland*, 1691.]

Sampson, George Vaughan. *Statistical Survey of the County of Londonderry*. Dublin, 1802. [Sent to Jefferson by his brother, William, cited below.]

Sampson, William. *Memoirs of William Sampson: including...a short sketch of the history of Ireland, particularly as it respects the spirit of British domination in that country.* New York, 1807.

Sidney, Algernon. *Discourses concerning Government.* London, 1761. [Original edition, 1683. An English republican, executed in 1683, whose writings were highly regarded by Jefferson.]

Statutes of Ireland in force in 1678. Dublin, 1678.

Warner, Ferdinando. *The History of Ireland.* London, 1763.

Warner, Ferdinando. *The History of the Rebellion and Civil-War in Ireland.* London, 1768.

BIBLIOGRAPHY

Ackerly, Mary D. and Lula E.J. Parker. *Our Kin: The Genealogies of Some of the Early Families Who Made History in the Founding and Development of Bedford County.* Lynchburg, Virginia: J.P. Bell, 1930.

Alexander, James. *Early Charlottesville, 1828-1874.* Charlottesville: Albemarle County Historical Society, 1963.

Averill, Gage. *A Day for the Hunter, A Day for the Prey.* Chicago: University Press, 1997.

Bailey, James H. *A History of the Diocese of Richmond—The Formative Years.* Richmond, Virginia: Diocese of Richmond, 1956.

Bartlett, Thomas. "An End to Moral Economy: The Irish Militia Disturbances of 1793." *Past and Present,* 99 (May, 1983), 41-64.

Bartlett, Thomas. *Ireland—A History.* Cambridge: UP, 2010.

Beckles, Hilary McD. " A 'riotous and unruly lot': Irish Indentured Servants and Freemen in the English West Indies." *William and Mary Quarterly,* xlvii (1990), 503-522.

Berleth, Richard. *The Twilight Lords.* New York: Barnes and Noble, 1978.

Birmingham, Stephen. *Real Lace: America's Irish Rich.* New York: Harper, 1973.

Blake, John W. "Transportation from Ireland to America, 1653-1660." *Irish Historical Studies,* 3

(1942-43), 268-280.

Bruce, Philip A. *Economic History of Virginia in the Seventeenth Century.* New York: Peter Smith, 1935. Two volumes.

Canny, Nicholas. "The Ideology of English Colonization: From Ireland to America." *William and Mary Quarterly (*series 3), 30 (1973), 575-598.

Carney, James. *Medieval Irish Lyrics.* Dublin: Dolmen Press, 1985 (original edition, 1967).

Casey, Daniel J. and Robert E. Rhodes, eds. *Views of the Irish Peasantry 1800-1916.* Hamden, Connecticut: Archon, 1977.

Chalmers, Harvey II. *How the Irish Built the Erie.* New York: Bookman, 1964.

Clemons, Harry. *Notes on the Professors for Whom the University of Virginia Halls and Residence Houses Are Named.* Charlottesville: University Press,1961.

Clover, Cecile W. and F.T. Heblich. *Holsinger's Charlottesville: A Collection of Photographs.* Charlottesville: Art Restoration Services, 1995. Second edition.

Coldham, Peter Wilson, ed. *The Bristol Registers of Servants Sent to Foreign Plantations 1654-1686.* Baltimore: Genealogical Publishing, 1988.

Coles, William B. *The Coles Family of Virginia.* Baltimore: Gateway Press, 1989.

Conrad, David Holmes, "Early History of Winchester." *Annual Papers of Winchester*

Virginia Historical Society, Vol. 1 (1931), 169-232.

Couper, Col. William. *Claudius Crozet.* Charlottesville: Historical Publishing Co., 1936.

Crowley, John, et al., eds. *Atlas of the Great Irish Famine.* New York: NYU Press, 2012.

Cullen, L.M. *An Economic History of Ireland Since 1660.* London: Batsford, 1972.

Curtin, Nancy J. *The United Irishmen: Popular Politics in Ulster and Dublin, 1791-1798.* Oxford: Clarendon Press, 1994.

Darst, H. Jackson. *Dublin of the Darsts: The Portrait of a Virginia Country Town and One of Its Families.* Newbern, Virginia: Wilderness Road Regional Museum, 1992.

DeGrazia, Laura Murphy and Diane Fitzpatrick Habestroh. *Irish Relatives and Friends: From "Information Wanted" Ads in the Irish-American* [newspaper], 1850-1871. Baltimore: Genealogical Publishing Co., 2001.

Dickson, Charles. *The Wexford Rising in 1798: Its Causes and Its Course.* Tralee, Ireland: Kerryman, 1956.

Donleavy, Kevin. *Dedication of the Monument to John Neilson.* Charlottesville: private printing, 1999.

Doyle, David N. *Ireland, Irishmen and Revolutionary America, 1760-1820.* Dublin and Cork: Mercier, 1981.

Dunn, Richard S. *Sugar and Slaves: The Rise of the Planter Class in the English West Indies,*

1624-1713. New York: Norton, 1973.

Durey, Michael, "The Fate of the Rebels After 1798." *History Today,* 48 (6), June 1998, 21-27.

Durey, Michael, "Transatlantic Patriotism: Political Exiles and America in the Age of Revolution." *Artisans, Peasants and Proletarians,* ed. Clive Emsley and James Walvin. London: Croom Helm, 1985.

Ellis, Peter Beresford. *Hell or Connaught ! The Cromwellian Colonization of Ireland 1652-1660*. London: Hamish Hamilton, 1975.

Emmet, Thomas Addis. *Ireland Under English Rule; or, A Plea For the Plaintiff*. New York: Putnam, 1909.

Emmet, Thomas Addis. *Irish Emigration During the Seventeenth and Eighteenth Centuries*. New York: private printing, 1899.

Fitzgerald, Robert C. *My Roots in Nelson County, Virginia*. Huddleston, Virginia: private printing, 1999.

Fogarty, Gerald P. *Commonwealth Catholicism.* Notre Dame, Indiana: University Press, 2001.

Forrest, William S. *Historical and Descriptive Sketches of Norfolk and Vicinity*. Philadelphia: Lindsay & Blakiston, 1853.

Gleeson, David T. *The Irish in the South, 1815-1877*. Chapel Hill: University of North Carolina Press, 2001.

Golway, Terry. *Irish Rebel: John Devoy and America's Fight for Irish Freedom*. New York: St. Martin's Press, 1998.

Gray, Peter. *The Irish Famine*. New York:
Abrams, 1995.

Greer, George Cabell. *Early Virginia Immigrants
1623-1666*. Richmond: Hill, 1912.

Gwynn, Aubrey. "Documents relating to the Irish
in the West Indies." *Analecta Hibernica* 4,
(1930), 235-255.

Hanson, Raus McDill. *Virginia Place Names*.
Verona, Virginia: McClure Press, 1969.

Hawke, George R. *A History of Waynesboro,
Virginia to 1900*. Waynesboro: Historical
Commission, 1997.

Headley, Robert K., Jr. *Genealogical Abstracts
from 18th-Century Virginia Newspapers*.
Baltimore: Genealogical Publishing, 1987.

Hodson, Peter. *Birth of a Virginia Plantation
House*. Richmond: Center for Palladian Studies
in America, 2012

Huffer, Donna. *Fare Thee Well, Old Joe Clark:
History of the Clark Family of Rockbridge
County*. Churchville, Virginia: private printing,
1991.

Hunter, Robert F. and Edwin L. Dooley, Jr.
Claudius Crozet, French Engineer in America.
Charlottesville: University Press, 1989.

Hurst, Ronald L. "Irish Influences on Cabinet-
making in Virginia's Rappahannock River
Basin." *American Furniture,* ed Luke
Beckerdite (1997), 171-195.

Inglis, Brian. *The Freedom of the Press in Ireland,
1784-1841*. London: Faber, 1954.

Jacob, Rosamond. *The Rise of the United Irishmen.*
London: Harrap, 1937.

Kinealy, Christine. *A Death-Dealing Famine: The
Great Hunger in Ireland.* London: Pluto Press,
1997.

Lawless, Joseph T. "Some Irish Settlers in
Virginia." *Journal of the American-Irish
Historical Society* 2 (1899), 161-166.

Lay, K.Edward. *The Architecture of Jefferson
Country: Charlottesville and Albemarle County,
Virginia.* Charlottesville: University Press,
2000.

Leyburn, James G. *The Scotch-Irish: A Social
History.* Chapel Hill: UNC Press, 1962.

Liam, Cathal. *Blood on the Shamrock—A Novel
of Ireland's Civil War.* Cincinnati: St. Padraic
Press, 2006.

Liam, Cathal. *Consumed in Freedom's Flame—A
Novel of Ireland's Struggle for Freedom 1916-
1921.* Cincinnati: St. Padraic Press, 2002.

Linehan, John C. "Early Irish Settlers in
Virginia." *Journal of the American-Irish
Historical Society* 4 (1904), 30-42.

Lockhart, Audrey. *Some Aspects of Emigration
from Ireland to the North American Colonies
between 1660 and 1775.* New York: Arno, 1976.

MacCarthy-Morrogh, Michael. *The Munster
Plantation: English Migration to Southern
Ireland 1583-1641.* Oxford: Clarendon Press,
1986.

Madden, Richard R. *The United Irishmen: Their*

Lives and Times. Dublin, 1858. Four volumes; second series.

Madden, T.O., Jr. *We Were Always Free—The Maddens of Culpeper County, Virginia*. Charlottesville: University of Virginia Press, 2005. (Original edition: Norton, 1992.)

Manahan, John Eacott. *The Cavalier Remounted: A Study of Virginia's Population, 1607-1700*. Charlottesville: University of Virginia, 1946. Dissertation.

McGee, Thomas D'Arcy. *A History of the Irish Settlers in North America*. Boston: Donahoe, 1855.

McGinn, Brian. "American Triumphs of 1798." *Dúchas* (Spring, 1998), Vol. 26, Number 2.

McGinn, Brian. "Jamestown, Virginia: The Irish Connections at America's Birthplace." *Dúchas* (September, 1999), Vol. 27, Number 3.

McGowan, Joe. *Echoes of a Savage Land*. Cork: Mercier Press, 2001.

McGuire, Edward J. "Thomas Addis Emmet, His Life and Triumphs and His Love of Ireland." *Journal of the American-Irish Historical Society* 18 (1919), 247-253.

McNeill, Mary. *The Life and Times of Mary Ann McCracken, 1770-1866*. Belfast: Blackstaff, 1988.

Metropolitan Record & New York Vindicator, January 20, 1866.

Miller, Kerby A. *Emigrants and Exiles: Ireland and the Irish Exodus to North America*. Oxford:

UP, 1985.

Miller, Kerby and Patricia Mulholland Miller. *Journey of Hope—The Story of Irish Immigration to America.* San Francisco: Chronicle Press 2001.

Moore, Virginia. *Scottsville on the James.* Charlottesville: Jarman Press, 1969.

Morton, Frederic. *The Story of Winchester in Virginia.* Strasburg, Virginia: Shenandoah, 1925.

Munter, Robert. *The History of the Irish Newspaper, 1685-1760.* Cambridge: UP, 1967.

O'Brien, Michael J. "Extracts from Virginia Church Records." *Journal of the American-Irish Historical Society* 18 (1919), 205-207.

O'Brien, Michael J. "Grantees of Land in the Colony and State of Virginia." *Journal of the American-Irish Historical Society* 13 (1914), 214-219.

O'Brien, Michael J. "Land Grants to Irish Settlers." *Journal of the American-Irish Historical Society* 24 (1925), 87-124.

O'Brien, Michael J. "Pioneer Irish Settlers in Rockingham County, Virginia." *Journal of the American-Irish Historical Society* 27 (1928), 46-54.

O'Neal, William B. *Primitive Into Painter: Life and Letters of John Toole.* Charlottesville: University of Virginia Press, 1960.

O'Rourke, T. *The History of Sligo Town and County.* Dublin: James Duffy and Company,

1898. Vol. II.

Quarles, Garland R. and Lewis N. Barton, eds. *What I Know About Winchester: Recollections of William Greenway Russell*. Winchester, Virginia: Historical Society, 1953.

Quinn, David B. *Ireland and America: Their Early Associations, 1500-1640*. Liverpool: UP, 1991.

Robinson, Philip S. *The Plantation of Ulster: British Settlement in an Irish Landscape, 1600-1670*. Dublin: Gill & Macmillan, 1984.

Schrier, Arnold. *Ireland and the American Emigration 1850-1900*. Chester Springs, Pennsylvania: Dufour, 1997. (Original edition: University of Minnesota, 1959.)

Scully, Paudy. *"I Forgive Them All": The Judgement of John Twiss*. Newmarket and Herxheim: private printing, 2007.

Shulim, Joseph. "John Daly Burk: Irish Revolutionist and American Patriot." *Transactions of the American Philosophical Society* 54 (Part 6, 1964), 1-55.

Simmons's Directory of Norfolk [1801, 1806].

Smith, Abbot E. *Colonists in Bondage: White Servitude and Convict Labor in America, 1607-1776*. Gloucester, Massachusetts: Peter Smith, 1965.

Smith, James Morton. *Seventeenth-Century America*. Chapel Hill: UNC Press, 1959.

Smith, Timothy D., compiler. *Wythe County Virginia—1870 Census, With Supplementary Lists and Tables*. Wytheville: Community

College, 1985.

Smyth, Jim. *The Men of No Property: Irish Radicals and Popular Politics in the Late Eighteenth Century.* London: Gill & Macmillan, 1992.

Stewart, A.T.Q. *The Summer Soldiers: The 1798 Rebellion in Antrim and Down.* Belfast: Blackstaff, 1995.

Stewart, Col. William H. *History of Norfolk County, Virginia, and Representative Citizens.* Chicago: Biographical Publishing, Co., 1902.

Stoutamire, Albert. *Music of the Old South: Colony to Confederacy.* Rutherford, New Jersey: Fairleigh University Press, 1972.

Sweeny, William M. "Virginia County Records of the Seventeenth and Eighteenth Centuries." *Journal of the American-Irish Historical Society* 30 (1932), 122-133.

Tucker, George H., ed. *Abstracts From Norfolk City Marriage Bonds (1797-1850).* Norfolk: private printing, 1934.

Twenty-Two Hundred Gravestone Inscriptions From Winchester and Frederick County, Virginia. Winchester: Historical Society, 1960.

Tyler-McGraw, Marie. *At the Falls: Richmond, Virginia, and Its People.* Chapel Hill: UNC Press, 1994.

Ulster Journal of Archaeology, Vol. XIII, Part 3 (August, 1907), 101-105.

Watson, William E. et al. *The Ghosts of Duffy's Cut: The Irish Who Died Building America's*

Most Dangerous Stretch of Railroad. Westport, Connecticut: Praeger, 2006.

Wayland, John W. *A History of Shenandoah County Virginia.* Strasburg, Virginia: Shenandoah Press, 1927.

Welch, James. *Killing Custer—The Battle of Little Bighorn and the Fate of the Plains Indians.* New York: Norton, 2007. (Original edition: 1994.)

Whelan, Kevin, ed. *Wexford: History and Society– Interdisciplinary Essays on the History of an Irish County.* Dublin: Geography Publications, 1987.

Whichard, Rogers Dey. *The History of Lower Tidewater Virginia.* New York: Lewis Historical, 1959. Vol. 1.

Wilson, David A. *United Irishmen, United States: Immigrant Radicals in the Early Republic.* Ithaca, New York: Cornell UP, 1998.

Wittke, Carl. *The Irish in America.* Baton Rouge, Louisiana: LSU Press, 1956.

Woods, Edgar. *Albemarle County in Virginia.* Charlottesville: Michie Publishing, 1901.

APPENDIX

We learn some intriguing details and background of another Irish political exile to the US, cited in the weekly *Metropolitan Record and New York Vindicator*.

Thomas Mulledy was "a native of Ballymahon, county Longford, Ireland. He left his native country in consequence of his political opinions in 1796 [sic]. He was then a young man about twenty or twenty-two years of age. Highly educated..., he settled in Pennsylvania, where he married a young lady of German descent, and...removed to Virginia, where he became possessed of a very extensive piece of land in the valley adjoining [the town of] Romney" in Hampshire County.

Later researchers have established Mulledy's birth as occuring in 1763, his death in 1849.

The *Vindicator* article says of this exile, "Here the old gentleman spent a long life, much loved and respected for his generosity and hospitality."(1)

Mulledy would have learned that Hampshire County had two Irish-born justices-of-the-peace in the 1790s, Cornelius Ferrel and Edward McCarty. Other Irish-born were making a local presence in that era. They carried names such as Casey, Riley, Mahoney, Dolohan, McKiernan, Murphy, O'Donnell, Fitzgerald, McCartney, and others.(2)

Tom and his wife Mary were involved in land transactions in Hampshire in the 1790s. Tom was elected to represent his county in the state General Assembly in Richmond (1804-1805). His will is dated January 30th, 1849, and he was buried at the Old Presbyterian Cemetery in the town of Romney.

Hampshire became a West Virginia county when set up in 1863 as a separate state from Virginia.

In Mulledy's era, this area of Hampshire County saw an Irish element of some fifty or more individuals. The ubiquitous civil engineer Claudius Crozet (he of canal, road, and railway projects) had established in the 1830s the Northwestern Turnpike, which ran through this area. The road-building crew had many Irish hands.

Endnotes

1. *Metropolitan Record and New York Vindicator*, January 20, 1866.
2. Hu Maxwell and H.L. Swisher, *History of Hampshire County West Virginia* (Morgantown: Boughner, 1887), p. 276.

CPSIA information can be obtained at www.ICGtesting.com
Printed in the USA
BVOW04s1617131114

374909BV00004B/10/P